With Two Oars

With Two Oars

Reflections on Sculling

by

William B. Irvine

Bent Skeg Press

Published by Bent Skeg Press
Dayton, Ohio
inquiries@bentskegpress.com

ISBN-13: 978-0-615-81426-1
ISBN-10: 615814263

For Jamie

*Thanks for letting me row so much
and then for learning to row
so we could spend more time together.*

*Oh, and this is probably as good a place as any
to inform you that I bought a boat.*

Contents

Introduction

Anyone contemplating writing a book on rowing is well advised to wait another year before doing so. During that year, the would-be author will, if he is paying attention, discover new things about rowing that he will want to include in his book. Not only that, but in response to his discoveries, he might change sides in one or more of the ongoing debates on how best to row. But of course, if the foregoing advice is followed, the book will never get written, and the author will take to the grave with him whatever he has learned about rowing.

It is with these thoughts in mind that I have written the pages that follow. In my years as a rower, I have learned a lot, but the most important thing I have learned is that there is always something new to learn—if, at any rate, you are thoughtful and observant. Investigating rowing is like peeling an onion: under every layer of understanding lies yet another layer. This means that besides being a wonderful sport to participate in, rowing is a wonderful sport to think about. It is such a paradoxical, counterintuitive sport!

When I learned to row, I had zero interest in rowing competitively. I rowed recreationally for a few years—rowed rather badly, in fact—before a very good rower took me under his wing, retaught me how to row, and introduced me to competitive rowing. I have since raced in a single, double, and quad,* and I have competed in both sprints and head races. Rowing a single, I have occasionally won races, but I have also come in last place.

---

*The boats used in *sculling*—the form of rowing in which each rower has two oars—are the *single*, the *double*, the *quad*, and (rarely) the *octuple*, with one, two, four, and eight rowers, respectively. The boats used in *sweep rowing*—the form of rowing in which each rower has only one oar—are the *pair*, the *four*, and the *eight*, with two, four, and eight rowers, respectively. Sweep boats generally also carry a non-rowing coxswain (pronounced *coxun*), who steers the boat and coordinates the motions of the rowers. There is, of course, no one-person boat in sweep rowing.

Most of the time I have ended up somewhere in between: I would therefore describe myself as being a "middle-of-the-pack" rower. My competitive career has convinced me that I am not a natural rower. I do not have a "rower's body"; nor was I endowed with the genes that confer superior stamina. Indeed, it seems to be my lot in life to be a rower who is trapped inside a philosophy professor's body.

I am proud to say, though, that these shortcomings have not prevented me from racing. My endeavors as a competitive rower have brought me into contact with some exceptional rowers, and I have done my best to take full advantage of these contacts. I have learned a lot by rowing with and against them.

I have also learned a lot by interacting with non-elite rowers, as I do in my capacity, at the rowing club I belong to, as Learn to Row instructor and adult coach. The best way to learn something, they say, is to teach it to someone else.

Learning about rowing, it turns out, is a lot like learning medicine. A medical student will learn much more from dealing with sick people than she will from dealing with healthy people. By dealing with sick people, she will learn how to diagnose various ailments and hopefully how to cure them as well. She will learn how medical causation works—how something that happens in one part of the body can have a profound effect on a distant part of that body: "That infected blister on your foot is what's causing your headache." She will learn that it is one thing to prescribe aspirin to alleviate the headache, and quite another to treat the infected foot that is ultimately causing that headache.

Along similar lines, a good rowing coach will possess the ability to diagnose a rowing ailment: "Your boat is constantly veering to the right because your left hand is reaching farther at the catch than your right hand is." And just as important, he will have a cure that the afflicted rower can both understand and implement: "At the catch, your left and right hands should be directly across from each other."*

---

*The *catch* is one of the four components of a stroke. It is the moment when the blades dip into the water. The other three components are the *drive*, when the rower pulls on the handles to propel the boat through the water; the *release*, when the rower lifts the blades out of the water; and the *recovery*, when the rower slides, with his blades out of the water, back to the catch.

Having compared rowing to medicine, I hasten to add that as a science, medicine is vastly more advanced than rowing. Ask three doctors how to cure an ailment, and they will probably give you similar advice. Ask three competent rowers a question about a specific aspect of rowing, though, and they are likely to give you three different answers—unless, of course, they have thought long and hard about rowing, in which case, the three rowers might give you *six* different answers. The first might tell you what she regards to be the truth of the matter. The second might tell you that, thanks to his understanding of the complexity of the issue you raise, he is of two minds on the subject and will therefore give you two answers. The third, even more thoughtful rower, might answer you by saying, "It all depends." She might go on to describe three subcases that must be considered to give a complete answer to your question and then give you a different answer for each of those subcases.

One thing I discovered in doing the research for this book is just how deep a subject rowing is. Pick any aspect of rowing, something you think is obvious; poke around, and you will find not only that detailed studies have been done, but that the studies in question often reach different conclusions. In what follows, I will not attempt to do justice to all the arguments that arise in connection with rowing. I will avoid some of the great rowing debates for the simple reason that I have not yet decided which side I am on. In other cases, though, I will not only take sides in debates but will share with readers my reasons for holding the views that I do; it is up to them to decide whether the reasons I offer are persuasive.

In the pages that follow, I offer very specific advice regarding technique. In offering it, I by no means pretend to be giving readers the last word, chiseled into stone, on how to row. To the contrary, my objective is to provide rowers with a foundation on which to build their rowing stroke. Depending on their anatomy and physical abilities, rowers should adapt my advice and thereby "personalize" their stroke. Thus, my overriding advice to rowers would be this: if doing things differently than I recommend in the pages that follow moves your boat better, then by all means, ignore my recommendations. Having said this, though, I would quickly add that the real test of whether your boat moves better is not how it feels to you, but how it performs in time trials.

Most rowers will disagree with some of what I say in the pages that follow, and some rowers will disagree with pretty much everything; we rowers are, after all, a contentious lot. It is my hope, though, that most readers will acquire something of value by reading this book. They might gain important insights into what happens when a rower puts blade to water and, better still, having gained these insights, they might find that their rowing is raised to a new level. What I have attempted to do in the pages that follow is provide rowers with the book I wish I had access to in my early years in the sport.

This is a book about sculling,* the form of rowing in which each rower has two oars. Although some of the things I say in the pages that follow may be applicable to sweep rowing, in which each rower has only one oar, such occurrences will be incidental; I readily admit to knowing almost nothing about sweep.

Furthermore, the primary concern of this book is sculling in singles. These boats are the tippiest of the sculling shells and therefore the most challenging to row. If you can row a single well, you will probably have little trouble rowing a double or quad, although it might take some time for you to learn to coordinate your movements with those of the other people in your boat. It is entirely possible, though, for someone who feels comfortable rowing a double or quad to feel quite out of his element rowing a single.

This book is not intended for novice rowers. In particular, I don't think people can learn to row by reading this book—or any other book, for that matter. They should instead take a Learn to Row class and then spend a lot of time on the water.

This book also isn't intended for elite rowers. At that level of rowing, success and failure are determined by the last few tenths of a percent of efficiency that a rower can extract from his stroke. In the Olympics, for example, it isn't uncommon for singles, after racing for seven minutes, to be less than one second apart, a 0.24-percent difference in elapsed time. My advice to elite rowers: find yourself an experienced and knowledgeable coach and then do as you are told.

Not all rowers have access to an experienced and knowledgeable coach, though. Indeed, many rowers, particularly at the

---

*According to the *Oxford English Dictionary*, the word *scull*, used in conjunction with rowing, dates back to 1345. The origin of this word, though, is uncertain.

masters level, have no coach at all. Or even worse, these rowers are plagued with too many coaches. The "coaches" in question are their fellow rowers who take it on themselves to offer helpful advice. The problem is that because there are so many different theories about how best to row, much of this advice will be contradictory. Any rower who tries to follow all of it is therefore unlikely to make much progress.

This book is written with these uncoached, undercoached, and over-coached rowers in mind. More generally, this book is aimed at intermediate and advanced-intermediate rowers who have rowed long enough to know what questions to ask about rowing. It is my hope that the pages that follow will answer many of these questions, as well as some other very interesting questions that had not yet occurred to them.

Those who coach competitive rowers or teach people how to row might also take an interest in what I have to say, inasmuch as the pages that follow might give them new insights into old rowing debates and new ways of looking at old questions, which in turn can help them answer those questions when they arise.

Part One

Foundations

ONE

The Importance of Technique

Take the strongest, most aerobically fit person in the world, put him in a racing shell for the first time, and push him off the dock. He will likely be upside down within three strokes. Teach him the basics of rowing, and he will row without flipping, but his rowing will be slow and awkward. Despite his strength and fitness, he will routinely be passed by lightweight rowers—and even *elderly* lightweight rowers—who move their boats not with brute force but with finesse. On having this happen, our hyper-fit individual might pull his oars even harder and faster in an attempt to keep up with them, and as a result his boat will, perversely, move even slower.

Rowing is an unnatural activity, and with good reason. Our evolutionary ancestors on the savannas of Africa 100,000 years ago walked and ran. As a result, our ability to walk and run is wired into us. No one has to teach us how to do it—although it is helpful to have an adult around when we take our first few steps. The same thing cannot be said, though, of rowing. Without instruction, people will be woefully inadequate in a boat, and even with instruction, it will require many, many miles of practice before the motions involved in rowing make it into their muscle memory so they can row "without thinking."

It is instructive to compare rowers with runners. The percentage of rowers who can run is vastly greater than the percentage of runners who can row. And although a track coach can assume that those who sign up for track will already know how to run, a crew coach, at the junior level and maybe even at the collegiate level, can pretty safely assume that many of those who sign up for crew *won't* already know how to row. Imagine how different track programs would be if coaches first had to train new athletes to walk, then train them to run, and finally start training them to run fast!

Another reason rowing is unnatural is that it is in many respects a backward sport. You sit facing the stern of the boat, meaning that although it is easy to see where you have been, it is hard to see where you are going. Likewise, you pull your oar handles toward you to make the blades of the oars move away from you, and to make the boat turn to the left, you pull harder on your right oar. Not only that, but some aspects of rowing, besides being backwards, are upside-down: you lower the handles of your oars, for example, to raise their blades. This results in confusion when a Learn to Row teacher tells a student to "lower your oars."

A COUNTERINTUITIVE SPORT

Besides being upside-down and backward, rowing is a counterintuitive sport. On one occasion, I was rowing in a double behind a person who was switching from sweep rowing to sculling. He was continually splashing on the left side at the catch, thereby spraying me with water. His torso seemed vertical in the boat, but I could see his left knee as he went down the slide toward the catch. I couldn't likewise see his right knee. I concluded that there was an asymmetry in his form.

I asked which oar he customarily rowed in sweep. "Port," he replied.*

"That explains it," I said. "You have a bit of a splash problem on the left. It's because you're sticking out your left knee as you come into the catch. This is probably a habit you picked up in sweep."

"What do you mean by 'a splash problem'?" he asked.

This response didn't surprise me. A splasher is generally the last person to find out about his splashing. This is because the splashing takes place behind him, where he can't see it and isn't affected by it. The person behind him, though, will have little choice but to become intimately acquainted with the splashes. They might go into his eyes and mouth. They might soak his hands so that he has trouble gripping his oar handles. When the

---

*If someone is facing the bow of the boat, the port oar is the one protruding from the left side of the boat. Rowers, though, face the stern of the boat when they row, so the port oar is the one that sticks out to their right. In the pages that follow, I will try to avoid confusion by simply referring to a rower's left and right oars, meaning the oars that stick out to his left and right sides, respectively, when he is seated in the boat. Rowing purists might express dismay at my abandonment of standard nautical terminology, but I suspect that they will have no trouble following what I am saying.

row is over, the splasher might be completely dry, while the splashee is thoroughly soaked. Not only that, but when the boat is inverted in order to carry it back to the boathouse, bucketfuls of water might come pouring out.

I know about splashers because I was, in my prime, a champion splasher. Indeed, I was the worst splasher I have ever seen or heard of. If there had been an Olympics of splashing, with the winner determined by who could put the most water in a boat in a 2000-meter row, I would have been a medalist. In my early rowing career, I soaked many people, and as a result, when someone now splashes me, I do my best to take it philosophically: it is, I tell myself, a form of karmic payback.

I explained to the splasher that because of the way he was rowing, I was getting wet. He glanced back and realized that what I said was true. "Oh, sorry!" he said. "Why is this happening?"

I repeated the short explanation: "It's because of the way you are sticking out your knee. Like I said, this is a habit that you probably picked up in sweep rowing."

After pondering this reply for a few seconds, he asked, "How could what my knee does make me splash?" This question is, to be sure, perfectly sensible. His knee doesn't hold the oar handle or even come into contact with it. Why, then, was I talking about his left knee?

I gave him a fuller explanation: "Because you are sticking out your left knee during the recovery, you are causing the boat to lurch to the left as you go into the catch, which is when the boat is at its tippiest. This triggers in you a fear of flipping the boat, so instead of having a leisurely, proper catch, you are in a hurry to get your blade into the water. As a result, your blade is too close to the water when you square it,* and this kicks up a splash."

I suspect that this answer struck him as a bit far-fetched; I know this is how it would have struck me, back in my splashing days. And I would have been not only puzzled but slightly offended by the implication that a fear of flipping was somehow causally responsible for my splashing. I would have denied that I had any such fear.

---

*Blades are *square* when they are perpendicular to the surface of the water.

Anyone who wants to row well needs to realize that the chains of cause-and-effect in rowing can be both long and circuitous. This is what makes rowing a challenging sport to master and, as I've said, a wonderful sport to think about.

Because rowing is causally complex, the solutions to rowing problems are often counterintuitive. Generally speaking, when people offer solutions to a problem, three outcomes are possible. The first is that the solution solves the problem, in which case it is a successful solution. The second is that the solution has no impact on the problem, in which case it is a failed solution. The third thing that can happen is that the "solution" is in fact a *counter-solution*: it makes the problem *worse*. Once we are aware of the existence of counter-solutions, we can find them in every field of human endeavor. Rowing just happens to be a particularly fertile field for them. In the pages that follow, I will examine some common rowing counter-solutions.

A FORM-INTENSIVE SPORT

Rowing is a form-intensive sport: to row fast you must row with good form. And what is good form in rowing? From the point of view of a competitive rower, it is the manner of rowing that most efficiently converts her power output into forward motion of her boat. Bad rowing form, conversely, fails to fully exploit her power output or, even worse, diverts some of that power to *impeding* the forward motion of her boat. Thus, the most obvious way to determine whether a rower's form is good or bad is to measure how fast the boat moves when she is using that form. And here we aren't talking about form that moves a boat fast for a few strokes but form that moves a boat over the intended racing distance in the shortest amount of time. Furthermore, the fact that Rower A is faster than Rower B doesn't prove that A has better form than B; instead, A might be stronger than B, and through sheer strength is making up for enough of her bad form to be able to beat B. If A improved her form, she would be even faster than she now is.

There are, to be sure, many factors that affect how fast a boat moves, such as rowing conditions, the aerobic fitness and physical strength of the rower, and the strategy she uses in rowing a particular distance. But if we hold all these other factors constant, *form is good to the degree that it makes the boat move fast.* Thus, if a rower could speed up her boat by using alternate oars on alternate strokes, *that* would count as good form; if she could speed up the boat by singing "Row, Row, Row Your Boat" as she rowed, *that* would count as good form; and if she could speed up her boat by having a long and accelerating drive, *that* would—and in fact does—count as good form.

Sometimes people resort to aesthetic criteria to assess rowing form: good form, they insist, will be beautiful to look at. I agree that good rowing will be beautiful rowing, but the beauty in question is a byproduct of rowing in a manner calculated to move the boat fast. Such rowing will be symmetrical, powerful, and graceful. There will be minimal wasted effort. This combination of characteristics will result in an activity that is a delight to behold, even though it is not the rower's intent to dazzle spectators.

It was the beauty of rowing, by the way, that first drew me to the sport. A well-rowed boat will display a wonderful combination of power and finesse. Even more beautiful is a boat rowed on glassy-smooth water. Spectators can then enjoy watching the rower and his reflected image rowing in perfect synchronization. And more beautiful still—indeed, my candidate for the most beautiful sight in all of sports—is a double or a quad gliding across glassy-smooth water, preferably at dawn, with mist rising and its rowers rowing as one. It is a sight that, although exceedingly rare on earth, is probably commonplace in heaven—assuming, of course, that there is rowing in heaven.

Those who care about boat speed have to spend what energy they have productively. At the highest levels of competition, they cannot afford to waste a single calorie of energy, not if they hope to win. This is why the coaches of these rowers are obsessed with form and why their athletes likewise should become obsessed.

Even at non-elite levels of competition, form plays a huge role. It is what will enable a smaller, less strong, less aerobically fit rower to prevail over her bigger, stronger, fitter rivals. One diversion at regattas is to guess before each race which boat is going to win. When I first started competing, I would watch rowers carrying their boats and base my guess on how strong and fit a rower looked. I have since switched my guessing strategy. Now I wait until rowers leave the dock and start rowing toward the starting line. I assess their form during those first strokes and choose the likely winner accordingly. It is a guessing strategy that has served me well.

Rowing form, I should add, is a transient thing. They say that you never forget how to ride a bicycle. You do, however, forget how to row, and fairly quickly. I live in a part of the world in which it is either impossible or inadvisable to row in the winter. We therefore get off the water in early November and get back on in mid-March. In those few months, our rowing form will have deteriorated. Even though we have rowed for years, we must re-learn how to row each spring. Thus it is that each spring I get to experience, at least once, smashed thumbs during the crossover portion of the drive.* This is something that in a perfect world I would have gotten out of my system as a novice rower.

Rowing form seems to be subject to what physicists call entropy: there are forces at work that will, with the passage of time, cause your rowing form to deteriorate. This means that if you ignore your form, you will develop bad habits. Your body will discover shortcuts that simultaneously make rowing easier and less efficient. To resist this phenomenon, you have to spend time and energy actively trying to improve your form. Stated bluntly, unless you are actively trying to row better, you *will* row worse.

It is useful for rowers to think of their rowing form the way they might think of a fine old Victorian mansion. The mansion in question will require constant maintenance, and if that maintenance is skipped, the mansion will fall into a state of dis-repair. It will transmogrify from something beautiful into something hideous. The same can be said of rowing form. Thus, anyone who wants to row well is faced with not one but two tasks. He must first work hard to acquire good form, and he must then work almost as hard to retain the form he has acquired.

Part of any form-maintenance program is not to allow yourself to row with bad form—not when you are rowing away from the dock, not when you are paddling during the recovery phase between sprints, not ever. As Charlie Doyle,† my first rowing mentor, used to tell me, "Each imperfect stroke you voluntarily take is a stroke you are giving to your competitors."

This same mentor taught me how important it is for a rower to learn to "set" his boat. If your boat has set, he used to say, rowing will be like dancing, but if it lacks set, rowing will be like wrestling. Let us therefore turn our attention to the concept of boat set. What is it, why is it important, and how can we get it?

Crossover is the interval in the middle of the drive and recovery when the butt of the left oar handle is to the right of the butt of the right oar handle.

†Charlie was an exceptional rower, who rowed first as a junior for the New York Athletic Club, then for Marietta College, and finally as a masters rower. He was also an exceptional human being. He died suddenly in 2007.

TWO

What Is Set?

Like most novice rowers, I was oblivious to set. That changed when Charlie Doyle invited me to go out in a double with him. It remains a mystery to me why he would have done this. He was a very good rower, and I was a very bad rower. Perhaps I was so bad that he took pity on me? Perhaps he thought teaching me to row well would be one of the greatest challenges that he, as a rower, could undertake? I'll never know.

After rowing for a while, he told me to weigh enough.* When the boat came to a stop, I asked how we were doing. "Okay," he said, "but the set needs work."

"What do you mean by *the set*?" I asked.

He responded by moving the handles of his feathered oars† up and down in opposite directions, thereby causing the boat to rock violently. I panicked.

"A boat with good set," he explained, "won't lean toward one side as you row along, nor will it rock from one side to the other. Instead, it will be perfectly balanced throughout the stroke. Set is very, very important if you want to row well."

"And our set isn't good?" I asked.

Weigh enough is nautical-speak for "stop doing what you are doing." It is correctly pronounced as a single word: *waynuf*. On the water, a coxswain might call out "Weigh enough" to get the rowers in the boat to stop rowing. It is an expression, though, that rowers also use on dry land, with varying results. On one occasion, I was getting separated from my wife in a moving crowd at an airport, and to prevent her from getting even farther ahead of me, I shouted out, "Weigh enough." Since she is a rower, she stopped walking, while the rest of the crowd kept moving, which is precisely what I had hoped would happen. On another occasion, though, I instinctively shouted out the "way enough" command to relatives who were about to crash into a wall with a table they were carrying. Since they were not rowers, the command had no effect, and a crash ensued.

†An oar is *feathered* when its blade is parallel to the surface of the water; an oar is *square*, as we have seen, when its blade is perpendicular to the surface of the water.

"Let me show you," he said. We started rowing. After we had gotten up to speed, he told me that on a coming stroke, he would say, "Pause," and that when I heard this command, I was to release my blades from the water, feather them, and move my hands to the "away" position—in other words, move them away from my body until they were over my lower thighs. I was to freeze in this position, keeping my blades off the water, until the boat came to a stop. The goal, he explained, was to see what the boat did when we let it glide.

He gave the command, and I paused. The boat immediately flopped to the left, and our dragging oars brought it to a stop.

"See," he said, "we don't have set."

I was puzzled: "But that's just what boats do!" I said this because it's what every boat I had ever been in had done when I tried to let it glide. Sometimes I could get it to glide for a bit before it flopped, but often the flop was instantaneous.

He rejected this assertion: "No, boats don't do that by themselves. In fact, a boat that is moving forward *wants* to have set. It *wants* to be level. If it doesn't have set, it is because the rower did something to ruin it. Blame the rower, not the boat."

"But I didn't *do* anything!" I protested.

He assured me that I had indeed done something. More precisely, I had committed the sin of "breaking symmetry." He explained that when you row, your body should be perfectly symmetrical with respect to the vertical plane that runs down the center of the boat, from the bow ball to the tip of the stern. What happens on your left side should be the mirror image of what happens on your right.

Lots of rowers, he added, don't row this way; they instead break symmetry. Maybe one knee sticks out asymmetrically as they move down the slide toward the catch, or maybe they reach farther at the catch with their left hand than they do with their right. In proper rowing, symmetry won't be broken—unless, of course, a rower is trying to turn the boat, something that can't be done without breaking symmetry. It is also permissible, he said, for a rower to break symmetry to recover from having caught a crab,* but in this case, the need to break symmetry is a bit ironic:

---

*Rowers typically catch a crab by feathering a blade before they remove it from the water. Because it is feathered, the oar will not want to leave the water; it will feel as if crabs are holding it under. Thus, the phrase "catch a crab" is syntactically backwards: you don't catch the metaphorical crab; it catches you.

one reason people catch crabs is because on the previous stroke they broke symmetry.

After letting this sink in, he continued his lecture. He explained that good set is important because good set in a boat makes rowing predictable. In a boat with set, the water will be in the same place, with respect to the rower, as it was on the previous stroke, and he will know where to find it when he goes to plant his blades at the catch. If a boat, instead of being level, rocks from side to side during the stroke or even worse, if it lurches to one side or the other at the end of the recovery, rowing will become unpredictable. Each stroke will be an adventure, with the water being in a different position, relative to him, than it was on the previous stroke. He will, as a result, find it difficult to establish a rhythm in his rowing. Not only that, but the unpredictable side-to-side motion of the boat will make him worry that the boat will flip, and as a result, he will start rowing defensively. He might, for example, start dragging his oars during the recovery in an attempt to keep the boat level. This "cure" for the boat's tippiness, however, will come at a price: the dragged oars will slow the boat down and maybe kick up a splash at the catch as well.

HAVING SET AND BEING LEVEL

It is important, at this point, for readers to realize that there is a profound difference between a boat *having set* and a boat *being level*: if a boat has set, it will be level; but if a boat is level, it won't necessarily have set. This is because there are other ways to keep a boat level than by setting it. Allow me to explain.

Consider the bicycle. Most people, when they first attempt to ride one, have trouble keeping it upright, and as a result, they resort to training wheels. But riding a bike with training wheels, their friends and siblings will tell them, doesn't really count as riding a bike. To *really* be able to ride a bike, you have to be able to balance it without training wheels. Notice that a bicycle with training wheels will be just as vertical as one without training wheels. The difference is in how the verticality is maintained, by balance alone or by resorting to mechanical means—namely, training wheels.

Just as there are two ways to keep a bike vertical, there are two ways to keep a boat level. You can do so by balancing the boat, in which case the boat will have set, or you can do so by resorting to "mechanical means." The means in question can take various forms.

A boat can, for example, have a broad and flattish hull, as do the boats to which my Learn to Row students are first exposed. These boats, thanks to their hull design, are extremely stable. They remain quite level when rowed, but not because of what my students are doing; indeed, the boats in question will remain level almost regardless of what a student does.* They play the same role in learning to row as tricycles play in learning to ride a bike.

When I move my students into boats with rounder, narrower hulls and thereby deprive them of the mechanical means that kept their first boat level, they are often dismayed: "The new boat is so tippy!" they complain. It usually doesn't take long, though, for them to figure out how to keep their boat level: they start dragging their oars on the water during the recovery. In doing this, they are using their oars as a mechanical means for keeping the boat level; more precisely, they are using their oars as impromptu outriggers. Thus, dragged oars play the same role in learning to row as training wheels play in learning to ride a bike.

The important thing to realize is that my Learn to Row students will have a level boat; indeed, it will be as level as the boats rowed by competitive rowers. But unlike them, my students will not have a boat with good set. This is because the levelness of their boat will be due to "mechanical means"—a wide, flattish hull in one case, and oars used as outriggers in the other. In order to *set* a boat, they must be able to keep it level *without resorting to mechanical means*. More precisely, they must keep the boat level *by balancing it*, the way a competent cyclist will keep a bike upright by balancing it.

---

*One thing we do in Learn to Row is teach a student how to get back into a boat that has flipped. I once made the mistake of using one of these ultra-stable boats in my demonstration. I had a student get in it and push off from the dock. "Now flip the boat," I said. When the student asked how this should be done, I replied, "Just let go of an oar." That is, after all, enough to flip most boats. She released an oar but nothing happened. "Okay," I said, "let go of both oars." She did, but the boat again remained level. By now, I was getting desperate. "Try rocking from side to side," I said. The boat stubbornly remained upright. "Okay," I said, "rock from side to side and then really heave your body in one direction." Finally the boat flipped, and the demonstration could continue. I should add that the boats competitive rowers use, if mishandled, want to be upside down as adamantly as this boat wanted to be right-side up.

At this point, a thoughtful reader might question rowing coaches' obsession with set. The reason set is important, as we have seen, is because it makes rowing predictable. In a boat with set, the water will be in the same position relative to a rower as it was on the previous stroke. This means that doing the same thing with his oar handles as he did on the previous stroke will have the same consequences for the boat.

This is the defense of set that coaches commonly offer, but in the form just stated, it is incomplete. What makes rowing predictable in the manner just described is the *levelness* of the boat. And while it is true that we can make a boat level by setting it, we can also make a boat level by resorting to what I have derided as "mechanical means." So why not resort to those means? Why not stay in ultra-stable boats with wide, flattish hulls? Why not drag the oars during the recovery? Indeed, why not put actual outriggers on boats to keep them level? If levelness is what you seek, this would be the easiest way to get it.

The answer to these questions is simple: if you don't care how fast your boat is, there is nothing wrong with resorting to mechanical means to keep it level. The problem with such means is that they invariably increase the boat's drag and thereby slow it down. In particular, dragging your oars during the recovery is like driving your car with the parking brake on, and as Charlie used to tell me, "You will get where you are going, but you will waste lots of fuel in the process." A boat that is level because the rower sets it will not waste fuel in this manner. Bottom line: to be fast, it isn't enough that a boat be level; its levelness must result from the rower's ability to set it.

LEARNING TO SET A BOAT

Rowers often leave my Learn to Row classes still dragging their oars. In Learn to Row, the primary goal is not so much to teach them to row *well* as to teach them to row *well enough to get themselves and their boat safely back to the dock*. I have done classes in which I set out with the goal of teaching rowers to row well from their very first stroke. That turned out to be an unattainable goal; until the generic rowing motion gets embedded in her muscle memory, a rower will have a hard time mastering the fine points of a perfect stroke. I have come to the conclusion, in other words, that before you can row well, you must go through a period of rowing badly.

Although I introduce my Learn to Row students to the concept of set, I do not expect them to be able to set a boat by the end of the course. When they graduate, they are allowed to transition to tippier boats, but I generally advise them to stay in the stable instructional boats we use until they can row them without dragging their oars and without splashing at the catch. Move to a tippy boat prematurely, I warn them, and they will set back their rowing progress. The dragging and splashing will become embedded in their muscle memory, and once there, it will be very difficult to expunge.

Almost without exception, my students fail to take this advice to heart. Some well-meaning rower will see them in one of the Learn to Row boats and say, "You should try one of the faster boats." It is advice that is hard to resist: if you want to row faster, it makes sense to row in a faster boat, right? The problem is that because they row the "faster" boat badly, they end up rowing slower than they formerly did.

Sometimes one of these rowers will subsequently ask me how she can get her oars up off the water during the recovery. My response: "Do you remember what I told you in Learn to Row about boat set? No? Well, then, let's talk about what you have to do to set a boat." I explain that the rower's real problem isn't dragging her oars but the poor boat-set that is probably causing her to do so. Dealing with the set issue, I tell her, will not only cure her oar-dragging problem but will dramatically improve her performance as a rower. I then volunteer to show her drills she can use to improve her boat set. I also point out that these drills will be easier to do in a less tippy boat than the one she is now rowing.

This, however, isn't what rowers want to hear. What they want is for me to have some trick up my sleeve that will enable them to "row clean" on their next outing—row, that is, without dragging their oars and splashing at the catch. If I had such a trick, I would happily provide it, but alas, I don't. What I instead have is a profound appreciation for the importance, if you are to row well, of learning to set a boat.

THREE

Symmetry

On the day he introduced me to the notion of set, Charlie said something that, although I didn't fully understand it at the time, turned out to be the most important—and most easily overlooked—thing about sculling anyone has ever told me: *"Good set is the backbone of good rowing, and maintaining symmetry is the source of good set."* I have since devoted considerable thought to this assertion and to the concept of symmetrical sculling.

To row symmetrically is to row so that the left side of your body is the mirror image of the right. To accomplish this, your torso has to be perfectly upright, meaning that a vertical plane that ran from the bow ball to the tip of the stern would run between your nostrils. Your left hand has to be doing what your right is, your left shoulder has to be doing what your right is, and your left knee has to be doing what your right is. (Sometimes, for added emphasis, I tell rowers that the pupil of their left eye should be as dilated as the pupil of their right.)

Symmetrical rowing, in the sense I have in mind, means something different in sculling than in sweep rowing. In sculling, rowers must individually maintain symmetry throughout a stroke: what a rower's left side is doing should be the mirror image of what his right side is doing. In sweep rowing, though, rowers must individually break symmetry if they are to move the boat: what each rower's left side is doing should *not* be the mirror image of what his right side is doing. Thus, sweep rowers who are rowing port oars will, at the catch, have both arms stuck out, asymmetrically, to their right. But although sweep rowers don't maintain symmetry *individually*, they can and should maintain it *collectively*: what the port-oar rowers do at any point in the stroke should be the mirror image of what the starboard-oar rowers are doing.

Not only should a sculler's body be symmetrical in the boat, but the blades of his oars should be symmetrical as well: his left blade should be directly across from his right, and they should be the same distance above or below the waterline. You might think that if a rower simply kept his body symmetrical and in particular kept his hands symmetrical, the symmetry of his blades would take care of itself. You would be mistaken, though. Allow me to explain why.

The Symmetry Principles

The sensible way to row would be with oars, the inboard portions* of which were short enough so the handles would easily clear each other in the middle of the stroke. This is how fishermen size the oars for their dinghies. It isn't how scullers do it, though. For example, I currently have my oars and rigging adjusted so that in the middle of the stroke, when my oars are perpendicular to the boat, my oar handles overlap by eight inches—about twenty centimeters—meaning that at the point of maximum crossover, most of my right hand is to the left of my left hand. (Elite rowers, by way of contrast, typically "load" their oars more than I do, meaning shorter inboard portions of their oars and therefore less overlap.)

I could avoid the crossover phenomenon by shortening the inboard portions of my oars enough to eliminate any overlap, but that would make it very hard for me to pull on my oars. There would simply be too much leverage—unless I also shortened the outboard portion of the oars, in which case they wouldn't be very effective. Thus, if you want a boat to move fast, your oar handles must cross over in the middle of the stroke. Fishermen in dinghies, of course, typically aren't interested in speed.

This means that scullers *can't* keep their hands symmetrical when they row. If they try to do so, their oar handles will collide on every stroke, and their thumbs will get smashed. This brings us to the First Principle of Sculling Symmetry: *it is impossible, when sculling, to keep your hands symmetrical throughout the stroke.* More precisely, it is impossible, when sculling, to

---

*The inboard portion of the oar is the part of the shaft between the butt of the handle and the *button*, the ring that prevents the oar from slipping through the oarlock. The outboard portion is the part between the button and the outer edge of the blade. By moving the button, a rower can vary the lengths of the inboard and outboard portions of the oar.

keep your hands both *vertically* symmetrical (with both hands at the same height) and *horizontally* symmetrical (with both hands directly across from each other) throughout the stroke.

What your hands do, though, affects what your blades do, and it is what your blades do that has the greatest impact on boat performance: they are, after all, what come into contact with the water. Ideally, your blades will be symmetrical. They will, that is, be both *vertically* symmetrical, with one blade always the same distance above or below the water as the other, and *horizontally* symmetrical, with one blade always directly across from the other.

To see why blade symmetry is important, think about what happens when it is absent. Suppose, to begin with, that a rower breaks *vertical* blade symmetry during the drive. One blade will then be deeper in the water than the other. This is likely to cause the boat to rock (and thereby ruin its set) or cause the boat to veer in one direction.

Now suppose that a rower breaks *horizontal* blade symmetry; suppose, in particular, that one blade is ahead of the other during the drive. This will likely cause the boat to "wag its tail": the stern of the boat will twitch from side to side on every stroke. It will do this because how much power a blade is delivering depends on where in the drive it is. Thus, if one blade is ahead of the other during the drive, it will, at any given moment, be applying a different amount of power than the other. This power difference will cause the boat, during each stroke, to rotate a bit in one direction and then rotate back. Tail wagging increases the drag of the hull and therefore wastes energy.* Thus, although a happy dog might wag its tail, a happy boat won't.

Besides being important during the drive, blade symmetry is important during the recovery. In particular, if the blades aren't directly across from each other, one blade will be farther from the boat than the other. This will cause the boat to lean in that direction, jeopardizing boat set.

This brings us to the Second Principle of Sculling Symmetry: *given a choice between maintaining either hand or blade symmetry, rowers should maintain blade symmetry.* In particu-

---

*If you don't believe this, sometime when someone is seated in a boat at the dock, grab the stern of his boat and pull it back and forth in the direction perpendicular to the boat to simulate "tail wagging." (It is a good idea, of course, to get the rower's permission before trying this maneuver.) The energy expenditure will be obvious.

lar, they should be willing to break hand symmetry if doing so will enable them to maintain blade symmetry.

Lots of scullers violate this principle. They know it is important that their rowing be symmetrical. Indeed, they might even be passionate about symmetry; it might be the reason they are scullers rather than sweep rowers. But the symmetry they tend to fixate on is hand symmetry, not blade symmetry, and the reason they fixate on it is because it is the obvious symmetry, the one that is right there in front of their eyes on every stroke. Scullers need to realize, though, that because of how boats are rigged, hand symmetry (during the non-crossover portion of the stroke, which is when such symmetry is possible) won't translate into blade symmetry.

This raises a new question: is it possible to maintain blade symmetry throughout the stroke? Is it possible, in other words, to maneuver the handles of your oars in such a way that your blades are always both *vertically* symmetrical (at the same height above or below the water) and *horizontally* symmetrical (directly across from each other) throughout the stroke?

In answering this question, we should keep in mind, to begin with, that unless you maintain horizontal hand symmetry, you *won't* maintain horizontal blade symmetry. This is because boats are standardly rigged with their oarlocks directly across from each other. With this rigging, any horizontal hand asymmetry will necessarily translate into horizontal blade asymmetry. Boat manufactures could get around this obstacle by building boats with oarlocks that are not directly across from each other, but they don't, and doubtless for good reason.

Thus, our original question of whether it is possible to maintain blade symmetry throughout each stroke turns into the question of whether it is possible to maintain blade symmetry by breaking only vertical hand symmetry. As it so happens, it is possible; indeed, I would argue that, given the way boats are standardly rigged, there is exactly one way to accomplish this feat. Allow me to explain how.

Rowing with "Stacked Hands"

To maintain horizontal blade symmetry throughout the stroke, you must, as we have seen, keep your hands horizontally symmetrical throughout the stroke. But of course, the only way for your hands to maintain horizontal symmetry during crossover is if they break vertical symmetry—if, in other words, they are held at different heights. And this is what I recommend that rowers do. More precisely, during the crossover portion of both the drive and the recovery, rowers should row with their left hand *directly above* their right.* They should row, that is, with what I shall call *stacked hands*.

The recommendation that rowers maintain blade symmetry by rowing with stacked hands raises an obvious objection. By rowing in this manner, they will maintain horizontal blade symmetry during crossover, but they will simultaneously break vertical blade symmetry. After all, if they row with their left hand higher than their right, their left blade will end up lower than their right.

This objection would be valid in a boat in which the oarlocks were set to the same height. In most boats, though, they are not. On many boats, the riggers are slightly bent so that the left oarlock is higher than the right, and in almost every boat, the oarlock heights are further adjustable with spacers and clips, so that the left oarlock can be raised higher still. What rowers need to do, then, is set their oarlock heights so that, even though their left hand is higher than their right during crossover, their blades will be vertically symmetrical.

Adjusting the oarlock heights in this manner, however, will have consequences for the non-crossover portion of the stroke. It will mean that besides keeping her left hand higher than her right during crossover, a rower will have to keep it higher *throughout the stroke*. In other words, her left hand will have to be higher than her right at the catch and during the drive. At the end of the drive, going into the release, her left hand will still have to be higher than her right, meaning that her left hand will end up at a higher point on her abdomen than her right does. Furthermore, during the entire recovery, this height difference will have to be maintained.

The most common mistake made by rowers who row with stacked hands is to restore vertical hand symmetry when not in the crossover portion of the stroke. Suppose, for example, that in the crossover portion of her drive, a rower keeps her left hand above her right, but suppose that as soon as she is out of cross-

---

*Realize that depending on how your boat is rigged and your oars are adjusted, your left hand could be *to the right of* your right hand in the middle of crossover. In this case, "directly above" will, in the middle of crossover, mean *higher than and directly across from*. The key thing is that the butts of your two oar handles will be the same distance from your belly button throughout crossover.

over, she equalizes her hand heights. Because her left oarlock is higher than her right, her right blade will end up more deeply submerged than her left, which in turn will create difficulties when she tries to release her blades. In particular, if she pushes her hands down "together"—pushes them down, that is, the same distance—her blades won't (in a level boat) come out of the water simultaneously. The resulting "sticky" release will slow her boat down or make it veer in one direction.

Likewise, suppose a rower, after leaving the crossover portion of her recovery, restores the vertical symmetry of her hands. As a result, she will arrive at the catch with her hands at the same height. But once again, because her left oarlock is higher than her right, her left blade will (in a level boat) be higher above the water than her right, which will create problems for her catch. In particular, if she raises her hands the same distance at the catch, her blades won't submerge simultaneously. As a result, her left-oar catch will likely be sloppy.

This last mistake, by the way, plagues the racing starts of many rowers. At the start of a sprint, a rower has to sit for an extended period with her blades planted at the catch. It is very tempting, while sitting there, to bring her hands to the same height. Do this, though, and one of two things will happen: either her right blade will end up more deeply submerged than her left, or her blades will be equally deep, but only because she is unwittingly tilting the boat to the left to further submerge her left blade. In either case, her start is likely to be a rough one.

Scullers, as I've said, tend to have a passion for symmetry, but unless they are careful, it is a passion that will get them into trouble. What scullers need to be passionate about is *blade* symmetry, not *hand* symmetry, and they need to keep firmly in mind that in order to maintain blade symmetry throughout the stroke, they have to maintain *horizontal* hand symmetry while, in a very controlled and constant fashion, breaking *vertical* hand symmetry.

Stated differently, *throughout each stroke they need to do two things: first, they need to keep their hands directly across from each other, and second, they need to keep their left hand higher than their right.* And by "throughout each stroke," I mean throughout *both* the drive *and* the recovery portion of each stroke. Doing this is the first step to maintaining the set of a boat.*

Someone might worry that any difference between the heights of a rower's hands during the stroke will disturb the set of her boat. It indeed will have an effect on boat set, but the effect in question is going to be minimal. Notice, too, that anything else a rower does to deal with crossover will ruin the symmetry of the oar blades, which in turn will jeopardize boat set. It can also cause a boat to veer. Rowing with stacked hands, then, is not a perfect solution to the problems presented by crossover; it is simply the least-bad solution. If you are going to row well, you need to be willing to look for least-bad solutions to problems and embrace those solutions when you find them.

Rowing with "Nested Hands"

After studying many rowing videos, I have drawn the conclusion that rowing with stacked hands is common but by no means universal among elite rowers. The most popular variant on rowing with stacked hands is to row with what I shall call *nested hands.* To do this, a rower, during crossover, keeps her left hand not *directly above* her right, but *slightly above and slightly behind* it—and by "behind," I mean closer to the stern of the boat. As a result, the two outermost segments (the medical term is *distal phalanges*) of the fingers of her left hand will "nest into" the innermost segments (the medical term is *proximal phalanges*) of the fingers of her right hand. In doing this, the rower is making a tradeoff: she is breaking vertical hand symmetry a bit less than if she rowed with stacked hands but breaking horizontal symmetry a bit more.

Those who row with nested hands will not need to have as much height difference between their left and right oarlocks as those who row with stacked hands, but they will still need *some* height difference. As a result, if they wish to maintain the vertical symmetry of their blades throughout the stroke, they must,

---

*I have described the advantages of keeping a boat level when you row. Research suggests, though, that many rowers, without even realizing it, cause their boat to tilt during the drive to help them deal with crossover. The tilting isn't much—only a degree or two. Whether this is the most effective way to row, though, is debatable. For more on this phenomenon, see Valery Kleshnev's *Rowing Biomechanics Newsletter* (July 2011). At the time of this writing, this publication was available online at www.biorow.com.

throughout the stroke, row with their left hand slightly higher than their right.

Rowing with nested hands raises questions that aren't raised by rowing with stacked hands. Those who row with nested hands will, as we have seen, break horizontal hand symmetry slightly during crossover, but what about during the rest of the stroke? Should they row so that their left hand is *always* a bit more sternward than their right? In particular, should their left hand be a bit more sternward than their right at the catch? Likewise, at the end of the drive, when they release their blades, should their right hand end up an inch or two closer to their abdomen than their left? Or should their hands be horizontally symmetrical at the catch and release, but switch to being horizontally asymmetrical going into crossover? And what effect will the horizontal asymmetry of their hands (whether it be a constant or variable asymmetry) have on boat performance? Will it cause the tail of the boat to wag? Will it cause the boat to veer?

I'm not saying that these questions can't be answered. I would like to point out, though, that those who row with stacked hands won't need to answer them. This is the main reason I advocate stacked-hand rowing to the students and athletes with whom I deal. Advocating stacked-hand rowing gives me a beautifully simple answer to the question of what they should do with their hands during the stroke: "Just keep your left hand always higher than and directly across from your right." It has the added advantage of being, I think, the best answer to this question.

I suspect that advocates of nested-hand rowing will be able to come up with interesting reasons for favoring their solution to the crossover problem. And indeed, during much of my rowing career, it was the solution I favored. But like I say, I am at present, for both theoretical and pedagogical reasons, an advocate of stacked-hand rowing.

Although different rowers will take different sides in the stacked- versus nested-hands debate, I think all sides will agree that a thoughtful rower will not only be aware that she has the option of rowing with either stacked or nested hands, but will have consciously chosen between these options.

Rowing with "Dancing Hands"

Another solution to the crossover problem—and not a very good one, in my opinion—is to row with what I call *dancing hands.* Rowers who use stacked hands will have no horizontal asymmetry in their stroke. Rowers who use nested hands will have some horizontal asymmetry, but it will be kept to a minimum and will be carefully controlled. Rowers with dancing hands, though, will exhibit, in their stroke, horizontal asymmetries that are both large and variable.

In one of the forms dancing hands can take, a rower's right hand will lead her left hand in during the drive; it will, that is, be closer to her navel than her left hand is. After the release, though, her right hand will shoot out ahead of her left; it will, that is, be farther from her navel than her left hand is. Later in the recovery, her left hand will catch up with her right. (By way of contrast, in nested-hand rowing, the right hand leads the left in during the drive, but the left hand leads the right out during the recovery, and the leads in question are slight.) All this horizontal movement of the rower's hands toward and away from each other makes it look, to my eye, like they are doing a little do-si-do; hence the name *dancing hands.*

Dancing hands represent an unnecessary break of horizontal hand symmetry and therefore of horizontal blade symmetry as well. They are likely to jeopardize the set of the boat, cause the tail of the boat to wag, or cause the boat to veer in one direction. They are fairly common in beginning and intermediate rowers, but even elite rowers can sometimes be seen using them.

In some cases, an elite rower's hands will dance throughout a race. More commonly, though, if a rower's hands dance, it will be for only part of a race. In some of these cases, the switch to dancing hands is involuntary: rowers do it because they are tired or distracted. In other cases, though, rowers switch to dancing hands on purpose, so they can slightly change their boat's heading. (They know that the horizontal asymmetries caused by dancing hands are one way to make a boat veer.) Having accomplished this goal, though, they quickly restore horizontal hand symmetry.

Air Space

Let us assume that a rower has decided to row with stacked hands. Given that a rower's left hand should be higher than her right throughout the stroke, just how much higher should it be? Enough so that during the crossover portion of the drive, there will be an inch or so (3 cm) of "air space" between the fingers of her left hand and the back of her right hand. Allow more space than this during the drive, and the left blade will go too deep in the water; allow less space, and a rower runs the risk that a slight rocking of the boat—the result, perhaps, of an encounter with a wave—will cause her thumbs to collide or cause the fingernails of her left hand to gouge the back of her right.

There isn't much danger of a hand collision during the crossover portion of the recovery: the blades will then be feathered and should be above any passing waves. It is therefore quite acceptable for the heel of the left hand to lightly touch the knuckles of the right hand during the recovery crossover. (Remember that because the wrists have been rotated to feather the oars, the heel of the left hand will now be occupying the air space that previously existed between the hands.) Alternatively, the knuckles of the right hand might lightly touch the shaft of the left oar. This will be possible if, because of the way the oars and rigging have been set, the rower's right hand is to the left of her left hand in the middle of crossover.

Indeed, if a rower has a problem with her left hand drifting high during the drive—meaning that her left blade goes too deep—she might make a point of having her hands come into light contact during the crossover portion of the recovery. Doing this can help her muscles memorize how far apart her hands should be, which in turn can cure the problem of left-hand levitation.

Let me end this discussion of air space by pointing out that rowers who row with nested rather than stacked hands will also want to keep air space between their hands during the crossover portion of the drive and recovery. In rowers who row with stacked hands, the air space will be between the fingers of their left hand and the back of their right; in rowers who row with nested hands, the air space will be between the outermost segments of the fingers of their left hand and the innermost segments of the fingers of their right.

ROWING ASYMMETRIES

As we have seen, good set is the backbone of good rowing, and maintaining symmetry is the source of good set. We have also seen, though, that rowers are forced to choose between blade symmetry and hand symmetry, and that the best thing to do, under these circumstances, is to break hand symmetry in order to maintain blade symmetry. And finally, I have argued that the least-bad way to break hand symmetry is to row with stacked hands.

This, I should add, is the *only* asymmetry rowers should allow. The rest of their body should be as symmetrical as possible. This isn't, however, what many rowers do. They instead have one or more (non-hand) asymmetries in their stroke, asymmetries that affect the set of the boat.

Some rowing asymmetries are constant in the sense that they are present throughout a stroke. A rower's torso might always lean to the left, for example, or although her torso is upright, her head might always be cocked to the left. Other rowing asymmetries can be characterized as variable: they are present during some parts of the stroke but not others. A rower might, for example, break symmetry only at the catch, by reaching farther with her left hand than her right.

Some of the more interesting variable asymmetries I encounter are found in sweep rowers who are switching to sculling. These rowers bring to the boat the asymmetries they acquired in sweep. I have already described one such case, in which a port-oar sweep rower tended to stick out his left knee going into the catch. In another case, I was rowing bow seat in a quad,* in which the stroke seat was occupied by an experienced sculler, and the middle two seats were occupied by sweep rowers, one of whom was used to rowing port oar and the other of whom was used to rowing starboard. On each stroke, I could observe a curious phenomenon: the torsos of the two sweep rowers would lean toward opposite sides of the boat as they went to the catch. As a result, I was able to see something that the bowman in a quad should never see—namely, the back of the stroke's head. In a well-rowed quad, the rowers' heads will line up, thereby placing two obstacles between the bowman's eyes and the stroke's head.

Asymmetrical rowing is undesirable because it makes the boat difficult to set—difficult, but not impossible. Consider again the sweep rower who, when sculling, stuck out his left knee going toward the catch. This is an asymmetry that would normally

---

*Quads, as I have explained, have four rowers, each with two oars. The person who sits closest to the bow of the quad "rows bow"; he is responsible for steering the quad and calling out necessary commands. The person who sits closest to the stern of the boat "rows stroke"; he sets the rowing rhythm that the other rowers must follow. This boat is sometimes confused with the sweep boat known as a "four." Both boats have four rowers, but in a "four," each rower has only one oar.

cause the boat to lurch to the left when the boat was at its tippi-est. But suppose the rower in question also leaned his head to the right as he was moving down the slide. If this second asymmetry perfectly counterbalanced the first, his boat would remain level. His rowing would look strange—like some kind of Rube Goldberg contraption—but his boat would undeniably have set.

There is, however, a far more elegant way for this rower to deal with his knee problem: stop sticking out his knee! More generally, the best way to deal with an asymmetry is not to find a counterbalancing asymmetry but to eliminate the first asym-metry. *Symmetrical rowing is the simple and elegant solution to many of the problems that confront a rower.** This is evidence, I think, that the gods of rowing, although they can be capricious and even cruel, must at some level love us.

When I started rowing seriously, I was frustrated by my inability to set a boat. I would try hard to set it and in doing so would only make the set worse. I concluded that the ability to set a boat is something that you have to be born with—or is maybe a supernatural gift from the gods of rowing.

I now know that setting a boat is a skill that any rower can acquire. Indeed, in the next three chapters, I will present a program for set acquisition. In the first stage of this program, rowers find the asymmetries in their stroke; in the second stage, they eliminate those asymmetries. The theory behind this pro-gram is that if you eliminate all your asymmetries, you will be rowing symmetrically, meaning that your boat will necessarily have set. In other words, boat set isn't the result of doing some one big thing; it is the result of *not* doing a lot of little things.

---

*Not all rowers have this solution available to them. For example, I know a very courageous athlete who rows despite having only one leg. She has, in other words, an asymmetry that *can't* be eliminated, meaning that the only way to deal with it is to counterbalance it with some other asymmetry.

FOUR

Finding Asymmetries

The best way to discover your rowing asymmetries is to have an experienced coach look for them. This coach might start her investigation by examining your hands while you are still on dry land. If you have blisters or calluses on your palms, she will deduce that you are clutching your oars, that the likely reason for this is that your boat lacks set, and that the reason for this in turn is that you are rowing asymmetrically. And if your palms are asymmetrically callused—with, say, your left palm being more hideously callused than your right—she might deduce that your asymmetries, whatever they may be, are causing your boat to lean or lurch to the left.

This coach might now turn her attention to the back of your right hand. If it has cuts and scratches on it, she will take a look at the fingernails of your left hand. If they are long, she might advise you to trim them nubby short, but if they have already been trimmed, she might conclude that an asymmetry in your rowing is causing your boat to tilt to the left early in the drive, thereby causing you to raise your right hand to prevent your right blade from coming out of the water, thereby causing the fingernails of your left hand to gouge the back of your right hand at crossover.

Having completed this boathouse diagnosis of your rowing, this coach will have you go out in a boat so she can watch you row and thereby discover the exact nature of your asymmetries.

EVIDENCE OF ASYMMETRICAL ROWING

If you have such a coach available to you, you are very lucky and should by all means take advantage of her. If you don't—and very many rowers don't—your next best bet is to have yourself videoed while rowing and then study the video. And whether you can get yourself videoed or not, you can self-diagnose your asymmetries *while* rowing. You can, for example, look to see whether your hands are symmetrical in the manner I have described and whether your knees are symmetrical during the recovery.

Besides observing yourself as you row, you can pay attention to what your boat is doing. Its behavior can provide valuable, albeit indirect evidence of asymmetries. We have already seen, for example, that if you fail to keep your hands horizontally symmetrical during the drive—if you fail, that is, to keep them always directly across from each other—it will cause your boat to "wag its tail." Thus, if you see your boat's stern twitching from side to side as you row, you can pretty safely conclude that there is an asymmetry in your drive—that one of your hands is ahead of the other for part of each drive. A little asymmetry will cause the stern of the boat to twitch slightly from side to side during each stroke; a big asymmetry will cause a few inches of movement.

A rower whose drive wags the tail of a single might not notice this same phenomenon when he rows a double or quad, and he might therefore draw the conclusion that, although an asymmetrical drive wastes energy in a single, it creates no problems in a bigger boat. This conclusion is incorrect, though. The asymmetry also wastes energy; it's just that the energy wasted won't be as readily visible in a big boat.

I should add that the best place to discover your asymmetries is in a single. Row in a big boat—by which I mean a double or quad—and the rowing of other people will mask your asymmetries. If, for example, you lurch to the left at the catch, they might start leaning to the right to keep the boat level. (They might also do this to prevent getting splashed by your left oar.) You will get the idea that you have the ability to set a boat. An outing in a single, though, will quickly disabuse you of this idea.

Another piece of indirect evidence that you are rowing asymmetrically is that your boat always veers off course in the same direction—to the right, let us suppose. This could be caused by a bent skeg,* an improperly rigged boat, or unequally loaded

---

*Skegs are the little "fins" at the stern of a boat; surfboards also have them. Unlike rudders, skegs can't pivot to turn a boat; to the contrary, their function is to keep the boat moving in a straight line. One question rowers often have is whether these fins should be called *skegs* or *skags*. The *Merriam-Webster Dictionary* lists *skag* as a variant of *skeg*, so a case could be made for using either name. The problem with using *skag* instead of *skeg*, though, is that *skag* is also a variant of

oars, but it is much more likely to be caused by an asymmetry in your rowing. The asymmetry in question could be a horizontal asymmetry: you might always be reaching farther at the catch with your left hand than with your right. (This might be because, coming into the catch, you are rotating your torso clockwise or bending your right elbow.) As a result, your left-side drive will be longer, and therefore more powerful, than your right-side drive, and your boat will respond by constantly veering to the right.

It is also possible that the asymmetry that causes you to veer to the right is a vertical rather than horizontal asymmetry. Your left and right hands could be reaching equally far at the catch, but during the drive, your left hand could be not just a bit higher than your right but substantially higher. As a result, it won't be just the blade of your left oar that is planted in the water; half the shaft will be submerged as well. By using both your blade and shaft to push on the water, you will provide more power to the left side of the boat than the right, and as a result, your boat will constantly veer to the right.

DRILLS TO REVEAL ASYMMETRIES

Another way to find asymmetries in your rowing is to do diagnostic drills. I have already described the *glide-at-hands-away drill* Charlie had me do. To do this drill, you get your boat up to speed and then pause during the recovery part of a stroke; more precisely, you pause at the point in the recovery at which your hands have moved to your lower thighs but your seat has not yet started down the slide. You freeze in this position, being careful to keep your feathered blades up off the water. You let the boat glide and see what happens.

Your boat might immediately flop to one side—say, to the left. This is indisputable evidence of an asymmetry in your rowing, and most likely the asymmetry is in your posture: your torso is leaning toward the left. To the rower, it might not feel like her torso is leaning, but unless it were, the boat probably wouldn't flop.

---

scag, which is slang for a cigarette butt or heroin. Thus, a rower who told his coach that he couldn't finish his workout because his "skag" fell off his boat would leave himself open to regrettable misinterpretation.

It is also possible, though, that the asymmetry in question is subtler than this. Suppose, for example, that you row with one blade deeper than the other—indeed, deep enough so that half of the shaft is submerged. Because submerged shafts resist being lifted out of the water, it will be harder for you to release the deep oar than it is to release the shallow oar. Consequently, when you push down on the oar handles to release the oars, the boat will tip in the direction of the deep oar. And when that oar finally pops out of the water, the boat will probably respond by rocking in the other direction. As a result, the boat will flop toward the shallow-oar side as soon as you start your glide.

This last case should make it clear that an asymmetry in one part of a stroke can have consequences, in terms of the levelness of the boat, later in that stroke: in particular, what happens during the drive can affect what happens after the release. It should also make it clear that body posture, although an important factor in keeping a boat level, is by no means the only factor. Thus, the process of finding your asymmetries so you can eliminate them will require careful thought and observation.

The glide-at-hands-away drill will help you detect asymmetries just after (or even just before) the release. Another diagnostic drill, known as *glide at the catch*, will help you detect asymmetries late in the recovery. To do this drill, you get your boat up to speed and begin your recovery, being careful to keep your blades up off the water. But whereas in the former glide drill, you stopped moving when your hands were "away," in this drill you continue down the slide and stop moving *just before the catch*. You sit there, *with your blades still feathered and off the water*, and see how far the boat will glide before you are forced to square the blades and catch water.

If your glide time is zero or close to it, it is evidence that your stroke becomes asymmetrical as you go down the slide. It could be that your torso starts leaning in one direction as you move toward the stern. Or maybe one of your knees starts sticking out to the side as you move down the slide, or your knees stay together but both start leaning to one side as you approach the catch. It could also be that as you come into the catch, your torso rotates, your head dips in one direction, or you reach farther with one hand than the other. Any of these things can cause the boat to go off balance near the catch.

It isn't uncommon, by the way, for people who can successfully glide at hands-away to have trouble gliding at the catch. This is because the moment just before the catch is the point in the stroke when the boat is at its tippiest. Allow me to explain why.

INSTABILITY AT THE CATCH

Boats are quite stable during the drive. This is because the submerged blades act as outriggers. During the recovery, though, the oars—if they aren't being dragged—will stop playing the role of outriggers, but they will still help a rower balance his boat: they will now act like the balance poles tightrope walkers use. The thing to realize is that the oars are most useful for balancing the boat when, in the middle of the recovery, they are perpendicular to the boat. At that point, they resemble a single balance pole. As the recovery proceeds, though, the oars transform from being the equivalent of a straight pole that sticks out perpendicular to the boat, to being a V-shaped pole that sticks out behind the rower. It is a transformation that, quite understandably, rowers find upsetting.

Imagine a tightrope walker whose nice, straight balance pole started kinking when he was halfway across the rope. Imagine that with each step he took, the kinking got worse, until finally, when he was a few feet from the end of the tightrope, the pole had folded into a sharp-angled V that stuck out behind him. This turn of events, we can imagine, would make him nervous. He might even abandon the pole, inasmuch as continuing to hold it made it, if anything, harder for him to balance. And it wouldn't surprise us if he started walking faster to make it to the safety of the platform to which the rope was tied.

Realize, though, that this is what happens to a rower on every stroke he takes. The farther down the slide the rower moves, the more V-shaped his oars become and the tippier his boat gets.* It isn't surprising, therefore, to see a rower rush to the catch so he can plant his blades in the water and thereby restore stability to the boat.

---

*A physicist would explain this phenomenon in the following terms. When the oars are perpendicular to the boat, the distance between the tips of the blades will be about 18 feet, which is the length of the two oars added together, minus the overlap of the oar handles at crossover. If the rower's oars are 30 degrees from the hull at the catch, though, the distance between his blades will be half of what it was. (This is because the sine of 30 degrees is 0.5.) The rower's "balance pole," in other words, will have shrunk in length from 18 feet to 9, and as any tightrope walker can tell you, a 9-foot-long balance pole won't be very effective.

On hearing this, a thoughtful reader might point out that going into the catch isn't the only time the oars are V-shaped; this also happens at the release. So according to the "balance-pole theory" I have just presented, the boat should also be tippy at the release. But it isn't, so perhaps there is a mistake in my theory?

I have two things to say in response to this observation. The first is that the V-angle at the release probably won't be as sharp as the V-angle at the catch: the two V-angles might be 90 degrees and 60 degrees, respectively. (By way of reference, a "completely folded" V would have an angle of 0 degrees.) As a result, the oars will have greater ability to balance the boat at the release, meaning that it will be less tippy than at the catch. My second, more important response is that the V at the release is occurring when the boat, because the blades have served as outriggers during the drive, is likely to be balanced. Holding this balance during the first part of the recovery won't be too difficult, even though the oars are in a V-position. By the end of the recovery, though, the boat, if the rower lacks the ability to set it, will likely be off balance. Just when he is in greatest need of a balance pole, he will have been deprived of one. So yes, the oars are V-shaped at both the release and the catch, but the latter V is more problematic for rowers than the former.

And while we are on the subject of V-shaped oars, let me stress how important it is, if a rower is to set his boat, that he keep his hands horizontally symmetrical throughout the recovery and particularly at the catch. Suppose that at the catch, a rower's left hand reaches 2 inches (5 cm) farther out of the boat than his right—not much at all. This difference in hand position, though, will not only be transmitted down the oars but will be amplified by them: thanks to the differing lengths of the inboard and outboard portions of the oar, a 2-inch asymmetry in the hands of the rower becomes a 4.54-inch (11 cm) asymmetry in his blades.* One blade, in other words, will end up significantly closer to the hull of the boat than the other, which will likely affect the balance of the boat.

And stranger still, the effect this hand asymmetry has on the set of the boat will be "reversed." You might think that stick-

---

*Oars with 88 centimeters of inboard and 200 centimeters of outboard would have an "amplification factor" of 200/88 = 2.27. Notice that 2 inches × 2.27 = 4.54 inches.

ing out your left hand farther than your right would make the boat lean to the left, since that is where the weight of your hand is. Realize, though, that sticking out your left hand farther than your right will cause the blade of your left oar to end up *closer* to the hull of the boat than the blade of your right oar. (Like I say, rowing is a backward sport.) Realize, too, that the blade is not only heavier than your hand but is, in effect, at the end of a lever, which increases its downward force. Thus, sticking out your left hand farther than your right will, perversely, cause your boat to be heavy on the right and will do so at the tippiest time in the entire stroke.

This is yet another reason why any rower who cares about boat set will want to keep his hands symmetrical (except for hand height) throughout the drive. More generally, if you want to gain the ability to set your boat, you need to hate asymmetries the way vampires hate sunlight.

PROBLEMS AT THE CATCH

Because the boat is so tippy at the catch, a rower who can't set a boat is likely to make technical errors during that part of the stroke. He might, for example, splash at the catch.

There are, it turns out, two distinct ways to splash. The first is when a rower, because he can't set the boat, drags his blades during the recovery. Because his blades are dragging, when he squares them for the catch, a splash is kicked up. The second sort of splash occurs when a rower, despite having kept his blades off the water for most of the recovery, gets nervous about the boat's stability as he nears the catch and touches his feathered blades to the water before squaring them, again kicking up a splash. I shall refer to this last phenomenon as a *touch-and-go catch*.

Most splashers splash predominantly with one oar—the one on the side that, because of the asymmetries in his rowing, the boat tends to lean or lurch toward. Thus, a one-sided splash is usually evidence of a stroke asymmetry. When a rower instead splashes sometimes on one side of the boat and sometimes on the other, it can be evidence that the boat is rocking during the stroke. This rocking, though, is probably the result of an asymmetry in rowing—most likely, a difference in the depth of the blades during the drive.

A rower who can't confidently set a boat all the way to the catch is also likely to make two other technical errors in the late stages of the recovery. One is that he will have a *premature catch*. In a proper catch, a rower will have slid far enough down the tracks that his shins are vertical (but not beyond vertical). He will, at that point, be leaning forward from the waist and his arms will be reaching out. As a result, his hands will be outside the hull of the boat when he raises them to catch water.

How far out they will be is a function of his *catch angle*. This is the angle between the oar shafts at the catch and the line perpendicular to the boat. Suppose, then, that a rower has a catch angle of 55 degrees. His oar shafts will be 55 degrees from perpendicular, meaning that they will, at the catch, be 35 degrees from the hull of the boat. At the other end of the stroke, there is what is called the *release angle*. It is how far from perpendicular to the boat the oar shafts are at the release. If a rower has a release angle of 30 degrees, his oar shafts, at the release, will be 60 degrees from the hull of the boat.

Add together a rower's catch angle and release angle, and you get his *total angle*, the angle through which his oar shafts move between catch and release. The size of the total angle will be proportional to the length of the drive. Inasmuch as a long drive is desirable—it is, after all, the portion of the stroke during which a rower is applying propulsive power to the boat—a large total angle is also desirable.

You can increase your total angle in two ways: you can increase your catch angle or increase your release angle. A rower quickly discovers, though, the anatomical limits to increasing the release angle: it is difficult to maneuver oar handles that have moved past his abdomen. Therefore, the best way to gain total angle is by increasing the catch angle—by reaching, that is, way out of the boat at the catch. Not only that, but research shows—somewhat surprisingly—that the blades deliver power quite efficiently when they are pointed bow-ward,* with a small angle be-

---

*After checking several dictionaries, I have concluded that *bow-ward* is not, in fact, a word. (Neither is the somewhat awkward looking *bowward*.) In the nautical world, if you want to say "toward the bow," you instead say *forward*. *Sternward*, by way of contrast, *is* a genuine word. A case can be made, though, that *sternward* ought to have as its opposite not *forward* but *bow-ward*. It is with this reasoning in mind that I will, in these pages, use *bow-ward* as if it were a real word, in the hope that if enough other rowers follow my example, *bow-ward* will someday be granted admission to English dictionaries, where it might one day be shortened to *bowward*.

tween the boat and the oar shafts—when, in other words, the rower has a large catch angle. It is for these reasons that a skilled sculler's catch angle will be considerably greater than his release angle.

As it so happens, the *average* catch angle of skilled scullers is 65 degrees,* meaning that their oars are only 25 degrees from the hull of the boat at the catch. Some scullers, though, have a catch angle of greater than 70 degrees. To attain these catch angles, a sculler's hands have to reach *way* out of the boat, and to accomplish this, the sculler might have to lean *way* forward at the waist. A rower, though, will have to be supremely confident of his ability to keep the boat set at the catch in order to do this.

Most rowers lack this confidence. As they move down the slide, they become increasingly aware of the tippiness of the boat and increasingly anxious to plant their blades, so as to steady the boat. This anxiety will cause them to catch "prematurely," and as a result their catch angle might be only 55 degrees—or even less.

A premature catch, though, will have a significant impact on the rower's power output. Suppose a rower has a catch angle of 65 degrees and a release angle of 43 degrees (which is about average, for a skilled rower), for a total angle of 108 degrees. This rower might pull his handles through 65 inches (165 cm) of "drive arc."† Suppose another rower, because he catches prematurely, has a catch angle of only 55 degrees, and the same 43-degree release angle, for a total drive angle of 98 degrees. His drive arc will be only 59 inches (150 cm) long. This is 6 inches (15 cm) shorter than the drive arc of the other rower. Six inches may not sound like much—it is approximately the distance from the base of your hand to the tips of your fingers—but it represents a 10-percent difference in drive-arc length, which is huge. This won't necessarily translate into 10 percent less propulsive power, but the power loss will be significant.

---

*For more on "average" catch and release angles, see *Rowing Biomechanics Newsletter* (November, 2001).

†Suppose a rower has a total angle of 108 degrees. If the inboard portion of the oars (the distance, that is, between the button and the tip of the handle) is 88 cm, the distance the handle tip will move through during the drive—what I am referring to as the *drive arc*—is given by $(108 / 360) \times (\pi \times 2 \times 88) = 166$ cm—about 65 inches. Lose 6 inches off that drive, and you have given up nearly 10 percent of your drive.

And even worse, by rowing with a small catch angle, a rower won't be fully exploiting a particularly important source of propulsive drive—namely, the hydrodynamic lift that the blades can supply. I will have more to say about this in chapter 8.

Notice that whether a rower has a premature catch is independent of whether he splashes at that catch: a rower can catch prematurely without splashing, or he can splash even though he doesn't catch prematurely. I suspect, though, that most rowers who splash will also have a premature catch. This is because both mistakes have the same root cause—namely, anxiety about keeping the boat level late in the recovery.

A RUSHED RECOVERY

Besides having a premature catch, a rower who has trouble setting his boat is likely to have a *rushed recovery*. Some rowers rush their recovery by moving down the slide at a high but uniform rate of speed. Other rowers start their recovery at a leisurely pace but accelerate as they get near the catch. In either case, it will be apparent to onlookers that the rowers in question are eager to finish their recovery. What will be less apparent is their reason for this eagerness: they want to plant their blades in the water in order to stabilize the boat.

Even though a premature catch and a rushed recovery are both caused by anxiety about the set of the boat late in the recovery, they are in fact distinct problems. The first is a *distance* problem: a rower with a premature catch won't get his hands out of the boat—*way* out of the boat—before his catch. The second is a *speed* problem: a rower will slide too quickly to whatever his ultimate catch position might be. It is possible, in other words, for a rower to have a premature catch without a rushed recovery (he would move slowly down the slide to his premature catch position) or to have a rushed recovery to a catch that isn't premature (he would rush down the slide to get his hands way out of the boat). A rower who finds it difficult to set a boat, however, will typically have both problems: he will rush to a premature catch—and then, to top things off, he might splash at that catch.

A rower with a rushed recovery will also find it challenging to row at a low stroke rate. Rowing at 20 strokes per minute, for example, means that he will complete a stroke every 3 seconds, which in turn means that his recoveries will have to be long and slow: if his drive takes 1 second, his recovery will have to last

2 seconds. A rower with a rushed recovery, though, will find himself at the catch long before the 2 seconds has expired. He will be sitting there at the anxiety-inducing end of the recovery, oars poised in the air, and will be unable to restrain himself: he will catch water. Instead of rowing at 20 strokes per minute, he might find himself rowing at a more conventional 26 or even 28 strokes per minute.

When you ask novice rowers to row at 20 strokes per minute, it is common for them to complain about how hard this is to do. They might even tell you that it is *impossible* to row that slowly. This is typically because they lack the ability to set the boat, and as a result, what should be the leisurely recovery allowed by a low stroke rate is instead for them a time of high anxiety.

Rowers with a rushed or premature catch will likely have what coaches call *bad ratio*. The ratio in question is the ratio between how much time a rower spends in the recovery and how much time a rower spends in the drive. One common piece of advice is that rowers should seek to have a 2-to-1 ratio—that they should spend twice as long in the recovery as they do in the drive.

While I agree that rowers should take steps to avoid having a rushed or premature catch, I think it is a mistake to fixate on any particular ratio number. This is because your ratio depends very much on your stroke rate and on how fast your boat is moving at that stroke rate. Row with a high stroke rate—as elite rowers routinely do—and strokes necessarily have to be completed in less time, meaning that there won't be much time for recovery, once the drive is finished. The ratio will end up being closer to 1-to-1. Likewise, row at a normal stroke rate but at very low power, and the boat will move slowly, meaning that the drives (if they are full drives) will take unusually long. The ratio will again be low.*

It is therefore a mistake for rowers to obsess about rowing with a particular ratio. Instead, they should develop a powerful drive. They should then figure out what stroke rate, given that drive, will enable them to cover their race distance in the least time possible. At the end of this process, they can, if they like, figure out their ratio. It will, I am guessing, be closer to a 1-to-1

---

*For more on rowing ratios, see *Rowing Biomechanics Newsletter* (March, 2003).

ratio than a 2-to-1. But whatever it is, that is the ratio that for them works best.

THE FEAR FACTOR

It is initially puzzling that a rower would want to get the recovery over with quickly. The recovery is, after all, the part of the stroke during which he gets to rest. A sensible rower will therefore want to spend as long as possible in the recovery.

What is it, then, that induces some rowers to overcome their innate human laziness and get the recovery over with quickly? There is only one emotion, I would argue, that is powerful enough to accomplish this, and that emotion is fear. Let us pause, then, to discuss fear and the role it plays in rowing.

In most sports, there is a fear factor. In baseball, it is a fear of getting beaned by a pitch. In horseback riding, it is a fear of getting thrown from your horse. In gymnastics, it is a fear of landing on your head. And in rowing, it is a fear of flipping the boat. To some extent, this fear is rational; it is, after all, possible to die as a result of flipping a boat.* Usually, though, flipping a boat won't kill you; it will instead leave you very wet but physically unharmed. This is why most people, given a choice, would rather flip a boat than get beaned by a baseball, be thrown by a horse, or do a face plant while dismounting from the rings.

Even when flipping a boat doesn't harm a rower physically, though, it can bruise his ego. A rower looks so stupid when, after piloting his boat gracefully for a mile, he ends up underneath that same boat. Then comes the humiliation of having other rowers watch as he attempts to climb back into the boat—only, quite possibly, to flip it again.† Most rowers, I would argue, fear flipping a boat not because they fear death but because they dislike humiliation.

---

*If you can't swim, flipping a boat can easily result in death by drowning. Even if you *can* swim, though, you can die flipping a boat. An oar can conk you on the head as the boat flips and knock you out; you can drown as a result. And even if the oars come nowhere near you when the boat flips, you can drown if you take an unexpected plunge into icy cold water. The plunge in question will cause you to inhale involuntarily, and if you are underwater when this happens, you will be well on your way to drowning before you fully realize that you have flipped your boat. This is a very good reason, I should add, not to row in icy cold water.

†It is not unusual for a rower who has successfully reboarded a flipped boat to take a moment to gather himself and, in that moment, let go of an oar. The boat will be quick to seize this opportunity and turn turtle once again.

Rowers are quick to develop their fear of flipping. The boats my students use in Learn to Row classes, although far less tippy than performance shells, are nevertheless tippier than canoes they might have paddled and far tippier than kayaks. This alone might strike fear into their souls. If it doesn't, it is almost inevitable that, in their early outings, they will catch a crab that causes their boat to lean precariously in one direction. An omen! Not long after that, they will either flip a boat or see someone else do it. By the time the course ends, their psyche will probably have been scarred.

A fear of flipping will affect how someone rows. In a severe case, a rower will be physically paralyzed by his fear: he will keep his body rigid in his attempt to maintain control over his boat, and in this rigid state, he will be unable to execute proper strokes. In less severe cases, rowers respond to their fear by rowing defensively. They drag their oars during the recovery to keep the boat level, or they rush to a premature catch. They also grip their oar handles tightly to ensure that they don't lose an oar. This defensive rowing will slow down their boat—a tradeoff they might be willing to accept. Ironically, though, defensive rowing can actually *increase* their chance of flipping. Here's why.

As a coach, I have had plenty of opportunity to watch novice rowers catch crabs. What is interesting is what they do in response: they tighten their grip on the handles of the rebellious oars. This means tightening not only the muscles in their hands but the muscles in their arms as well. They aren't going to let *that* happen again. They are going to show the oars who is in charge!

As a result of all this "muscling," they might start pulling the button of the oar away from the oarlock. You can hear a *thunk* noise on every stroke, as the button again comes into contact with the oarlock. By muscling their oars, they might also prevent their blades from going to the proper angle. As a result, they quickly catch another crab. (A rowing maxim: *crabs beget crabs.*) It is then that I deliver my little speech about the astonishing intelligence of oars: "Oars are smarter than rowers," I tell them, and I go on to explain how this could possibly be.

Oars "know" the angle at which their blades should be during each part of the stroke. The "brain" in which the oars store this knowledge is located in the flat surfaces of the oar collars, which fit into the precisely-angled flat surfaces of the oarlocks. In particular, the oars know the angle that will allow the blades, during the recovery, to glide over the surface of the water. If this angle is off by a bit, the blades will instead catch the surface and dive under. The oars also know the angle the blades must be at during the drive. If the oars have been under-rotated at the catch, so that they are "cocked"—meaning less than square to the water—pulling on the handle will once again cause the blades to dive.

A diving blade, though, is likely to catch a crab, and if the rower panics trying to get the problematic blade back to the surface, he can flip his boat. Thus, when a rower grips his handles tightly to prevent his boat from flipping, he makes his oars go stupid, and this can have the effect of *increasing* the chance that his boat will flip.

Rowers can also make their oars go stupid by putting them into reversed oarlocks—by putting them, that is, into oarlocks that point bow-ward instead of sternward. This will slightly change the angles of the squared blades with respect to the water and will thereby cause them to dive in a most disconcerting manner during the drive. Inadvertently reverse your oarlocks, and until you discover your mistake, you will be a pathetic site: a competent rower who suddenly is catching crabs on every stroke.

Gripping the oar handles in response to a crab is, by the way, a wonderful example of what I have called a *counter-solution*: it "solves" a problem in a manner that only makes that problem worse. Why, then, would anyone choose such a solution? Because it is the obvious solution, the one that clearly ought to work—except that it doesn't.

One reason rowing is a difficult sport to teach is because it is home to so many counter-solutions. Tell a rower who has just lost an oar by catching a crab that he can reduce his chance of catching crabs by holding his oars more loosely, and he will think you are crazy.

But I digress. In this chapter, I have described some of the ways a rower can discover the asymmetries in his rowing so he can eliminate them and thereby acquire the ability to set a boat. I have also broached the subject of fear—more precisely, the fear rowers have of flipping their boat. This fear, I have suggested, can have a considerable negative impact on their rowing. Let us, therefore, turn our attention to fear. In the next chapter, I will describe drills rowers can do to elicit their fear of flipping so they can desensitize themselves to it.

FIVE

Confronting the Fear of Flipping

I am convinced that a fear of flipping afflicts many rowers. Indeed, I would argue that at the beginning and even at the intermediate level, *most mistakes in rowing technique are ultimately attributable to a fear of flipping*. Prominent among these mistakes are dragged oars during the recovery, a rushed recovery, a premature catch, and a splash at the catch. I would also argue that many coaches underestimate the role "flipophobia" plays in rowing. This might be because they themselves were never afflicted by the disease. Alternatively, they might have felt its touch when they first started rowing, but that was so long ago that they have forgotten what it is like to row in the grip of fear. In either case, they will find it difficult to appreciate the extent to which a fear of flipping can distort rowing technique, particularly in those who row singles.

Fortunately for coaches, there is a "litmus test" for flipophobia. If a rower is dragging her oars during the recovery or splashing at the catch, it might be because she fears flipping and because this fear prevents her from getting her blades up off the water. To find out if this is indeed the case, a coach need only instruct her to hold her hands two inches (five cm) lower during the recovery and at the catch. If the rower follows these instructions, it is evidence that she is not flipophobic—or at worst only mildly so. If she doesn't follow these instructions, though, the coach should not assume that she is being rebellious. To the contrary, she probably isn't following them because she *can't* follow them. Her fear of flipping is holding her hostage. No matter how much she wants to lower her hands, her fear of flipping simply won't let them descend.

Unless a coach can help rowers overcome their fear of flipping, it will be exceedingly difficult for them to overcome the technical mistakes to which this fear gives rise. A coach might "cure" one mistake only to have it transmogrify into another. Suppose, for example, that a coach convinces a rower to keep her oars off the water during the recovery. The rower in question, without even realizing that she is doing so, might start catching prematurely so she can get her blades into the water in time to prevent the boat from flipping. One technical error will have been traded for another.

Sometimes a rowing problem has a dual nature: besides being a problem in its own right, it is a symptom of another problem. I would offer splashing at the catch as an example of this phenomenon. An effective coach, when presented with one of these dual-nature problems, will address the root problem, knowing that if this problem can be resolved, the other problem will take care of itself. Thus, cure a rower's flipophobia, and you will cure her splashing as well; fail to cure her flipophobia, though, and you will find it very difficult to overcome her splashing.

Even if a rower passes the above test for flipophobia, her concern about the possibility of flipping might negatively impact her rowing. In particular, she might lack the confidence required to really reach at the catch. Or when rowing in difficult conditions—with, say, wind or chop—she might start rowing conservatively. In order for her to reach her full potential as a rower, she will have to eliminate this last residue of fear. Let us, therefore, turn our attention to steps rowers can take to overcome flipophobia.

OVERCOMING FEAR

Fear can be a good thing. A fear of death, for example, is a wonderfully useful fear. It will prevent us from doing many foolish things, such as trying to fly by jumping off a bridge and flapping our arms. Other fears, though, are a hindrance to our functioning as human beings, inasmuch as they restrict our freedom in important ways. A fear of public speaking, for example, can limit our advancement in our chosen profession, and a fear of rejection can prevent us from forming social relationships.

If we are afflicted by such fears, how can we overcome them? One way is to desensitize ourselves to the thing we fear by repeatedly exposing ourselves to it. Thus, someone who fears speaking in public should go out of his way to speak publicly, at first in front of small and friendly audiences. And someone who fears social rejection should go out of his way to meet other people.

In conjunction with this last point, consider the desensitization program undertaken by psychologist Albert Ellis. As a young man, he was afraid to talk to women, which in turn made it very difficult for him to date them. He dealt with this fear by setting for himself the assignment of talking to a hundred women he didn't know. Every day for a month, he went to the Bronx Botanical Garden and approached the women he saw to engage in innocent conversation. Some of the women just walked away—the rejection he feared. But many more did talk to him for a while, and one even agreed to go on a date with him. Sad to say, she didn't show up, but that wasn't really the point. By then, Ellis had largely overcome his fear of talking to women. He had taught himself that being rejected by a woman isn't the end of the world.

Suppose that what someone fears is not speaking in public or meeting women, but flipping a boat. The most obvious thing he can do, as part of a desensitization program, is to flip a boat on purpose—preferably under controlled circumstances, in which the water is warm and calm, and others can help him if the exercise goes awry.* He will discover that although it isn't fun to flip a boat, it is something he can deal with. Not only will he have confronted the bogeyman that has been chasing him, but he will have wrestled this creature to the ground and pummeled him into submission.

Another very useful, albeit less dramatic way to deal with a fear of flipping is not to *actually* flip a boat but to put ourselves into situations in which our boat *might* flip. By doing this, we will elicit the fear that we are trying to overcome so that we can practice dealing with that fear. *Tap drills* are a great way to do this.

Whereas the glide drills described earlier are done in a moving boat, tap drills, also known as *dip drills*, are done in a stationary boat. In the *tap-at-hands-away drill*, a rower sits upright in the boat, at "hands away" position, with legs fully stretched out. His arms are extended, and his hands are over his lower thighs. He squares the blades of his oars and lowers them until they find their *flotation depth*, the depth they would be at if the rower were to release his oar handles—something, I should add, that the rower should *not* do if he wants to keep his boat up-

---

*Indeed, this is arguably something that rowers should be forced to do in their Learn to Row class. Given that capsizing is a fact of rowing life, rowers need to learn how to get back into a flipped boat.

right. At this depth, the top edges of the blades will be about an inch above the waterline.

To do the tap-at-hands-away drill, the rower now starts "tapping" his blades—causing them, that is, to repeatedly bob into and out of the water. At the bottom of each bob, they will be at flotation depth, and at the top of each bob, they will be *completely* out of the water.

To be able to do this drill, the rower will have to stay visually focused: he will have to stare fixedly at a focal point. This is also what he needs to do while rowing, if he is to have any chance at all of setting his boat. Allow me, therefore, to digress to talk about focus.

VISUAL FOCUS

A visually focused rower will stare at the point on the water-land horizon that is directly over the stern of the boat. This means that as his boat turns, his focal point will have to change. A rower's focal point might end up being a rock, a tree, or a bush at water's edge.

Sometimes, for emphasis, I tell my students and athletes that they should be looking not just at the bush on the bank behind their boat, but at a single leaf on that bush. This Zen-like feat is admittedly difficult, and I don't really expect them to do it. By talking this way, I hope to impress on them the importance of not merely *looking at* their focal point but *staring at it intently*. I am also trying to impress on them the importance of *not* looking at a variety of other things that might claim their attention, including their feet, their stroke-rate monitor, the stern deck of their boat, the water behind their boat, the blades of their oars, and those ducks over yonder. They should be visually oblivious to all these things.

If an athlete questions the importance of visual focus, I invite him to watch videos of Olympic rowers. Although these rowers are superb in their ability to set a boat (otherwise, they wouldn't be in the Olympics), when they are racing, they stare at their focal point with laser-like intensity. Indeed, one almost expects the poor bush they have chosen as their visual focus to burst into flames as a result of being stared at so hard.

Visual focus is important because wandering or misdirected eyes are ruinous to the set of a boat. They interfere with the operation of the body's automatic balancing mechanism. This mechanism also comes into play when riding a bicycle. When I was a child, I had trouble learning to ride a bike until someone told me to stop looking at the ground as I rode and to instead look out at the road before me. It worked like a charm, and it is advice that I have since passed on to the children I have taught to ride, with the same remarkable effect.

Rowers who have rowing problems often try to solve them by looking at their source. In particular, someone having trouble with the tap-at-hands-away drill might start looking at his blades going into and out of the water. The temptation to do this is quite understandable, but giving in to this temptation only makes the drill that much more challenging. (Looking at your blades while doing this drill is therefore another example of a counter-solution.) If the rower instead starts staring at his focal point, he might find that, as if by magic, his problem goes away.

A rower who is having trouble balancing a boat cannot afford to interfere with his automatic balance mechanism. To the contrary, he needs all the help he can get. So, an important first step in learning how to set a boat is learning how to focus visually. But of all the things you must do to learn to set a boat, this is far and away the easiest. To be visually focused, all you need to do is not let your eyes wander. It is a task, in other words, that is accomplished by *not* doing something. How hard can that be?

IN PRAISE OF MIRRORS

Let me pause here to offer a few words of praise to the use of mirrors when rowing. If you are rowing a single or rowing bow in a bigger boat, it is impossible for you to stare constantly at the focal point on the water-land horizon. This is because you need to be steering the boat, and to steer it in a sensible manner, you need to look where you are going—you need, as rowers say, to "look ahead."* Most rowers do this by turning their heads around. This, I should add, is a radically asymmetrical action, one that can easily ruin the set of the boat. This means that someone who wants to set the boat he is steering has to figure out how to look ahead in a minimally disruptive manner.

---

*This terminology is backwards, of course, since you "look ahead" by looking behind you, which is where the bow of the boat is.

If you are going to look over your shoulder, the standard advice is to do it during the drive. This is when the boat is most stable (because it has, in effect, two outriggers). There are, however, two drawbacks to looking ahead in this manner. The first is that unless your neck is unusually flexible, you will need to turn your shoulders when you look, and this will affect your drive and thereby might affect the direction your boat is moving. It is ironic that the act of looking ahead to insure that you are rowing in a straight line can cause your boat to go off course.

Even if a rower gets good at looking over his shoulder during the drive without causing his boat to veer, he will be faced with another problem. Looking ahead in this manner won't give him much time—at best half a second—to look ahead. He is forced to take a mental snapshot of what he sees. As a result, he might be forced to take additional "snapshots" before he feels confident enough about what lies ahead to plan his course. (This is particularly true in head racing, when the rower is looking for the next buoy, which might be quite small and hundreds of meters away.)

Sometimes rowers try to extend the duration of over-the-shoulder looks. Instead of glancing during the drive, they pause at the release to give the water ahead a good long stare. Doing this, though, will slow the boat down. It will, after all, lengthen the amount of time in which they aren't applying propulsive power to the boat, and if they drag their oars to steady the boat while they are looking, it will only make things worse.

So what is a rower to do? How can you minimize the negative impact that looking ahead will have on your boat? The answer is simple: use a mirror. These rear-view mirrors come in various forms. Some attach to your eyeglasses or sunglasses. Some attach to sweatbands. The one I currently use is attached to the right side (I have a dominant right eye) of the visor of the hat I wear to keep the sun and sweat out of my eyes. My mirror is rectangular in shape, and I set it so that it floats in my visual field the way a kite would float in the sky, with its corners at the top and bottom and on the two sides. I adjust it so that I can see the bow ball of my boat in the bottom corner of the mirror and see part of my ear in the inside corner. Then, by glancing to the right and without turning my head at all, I can get a very complete picture of what lies ahead.

The important thing is that this glance has zero impact on the symmetry of my rowing. Not only that, but it enables me to take long looks at what lies ahead. Instead of taking a snapshot, I can, in effect, take a video. Indeed, I can look ahead for an entire stroke—or for many strokes in succession—without breaking symmetry.

Although I *can* take extended looks, I have found that it is risky to do so. The set of the boat can suffer, and crabs can get caught. This is particularly true in a single. Thus, the best time to look ahead when you use a mirror is the same as it is when you lack one—during the drive, when the boat is most stable.

The case for using a mirror is so compelling that it is surprising that there are rowers who don't use one.* In the case of some rowers, it seems to be a matter of principle not to use them. I am uncertain of what the principle in question could possibly be. Other rowers have told me that they tried a mirror but had trouble getting used to it, and so gave up trying. This is a strange thing to hear from someone engaged in an activity—namely, sitting backwards in a boat in order to propel it forward with special nine-foot-long sticks—that takes years to get used to.

I knew the first time I used a mirror that it was worth using. It took several rows for me to feel comfortable using it. And even after using it for several months, I would occasionally misuse it: I would forget that the mirror reverses images and might, therefore, go through the left arch of a bridge when I had intended to go through the right. After a year, though, I was so used to rowing with a mirror that I had become dependent on one. If I forgot my mirror-hat when I went for a row, I would find myself glancing to the right side of my visual field to see where I was going, only to see the water beside the stern deck of my boat.

Some rowers—in particular, those who regard themselves as purists—might criticize me for having allowed myself to become dependent on a device like a mirror. In response to this criticism, I would reply that it is only one of many rowing devices on which I am dependent. To row effectively, for example, I require a seat that slides and oars with flat-sided collars that take the guesswork out of squaring and feathering my blades. It is difficult to see how someone can, on grounds of principle, eschew mirrors and not eschew these other "devices" as well.

---

*The exceptions would be those rowers who, because they never row singles or never row bow in a bigger boat, never need to know where their boat is going. Likewise, those who row in buoyed straight-line courses can navigate by looking back at the buoys behind them. But even then, a mirror can come in handy in traveling to the buoyed course and afterwards traveling back to the dock, and during the race, in dealing with a boat that might have strayed into their lane.

And let me make one last comment about mirrors. Ideally, rowers who look over their shoulder to navigate will alternate between shoulders. This way, they will get a full view of what lies ahead. Mirrors have the downside of having the blind spot created by the rower's head. This blind spot, though, is easy enough to overcome. If a rower's mirror is mounted on the right, and he wants to see what is on the left side of his boat up ahead, he need only turn his head a bit to the right. Doing this will have a far smaller impact on boat set than the head-turn that would be required if he lacked a mirror.

ROWING WITH YOUR EARS

Once I tell students and athletes not to look at whatever is giving them trouble but to stare at their focal point instead, they ask the obvious question: "If I am staring at some bush on the bank, how can I observe my mistakes so I can correct them?" I respond to this question by pointing out that their eyes aren't the only observational tool they have at their disposal; they have their ears as well.

A well-rowed boat makes very little sound. Row with bad form, though, and the noise level starts to rise. Another way to think of it is that the boat will start talking to you. It will give you suggestions about what you are doing wrong.

Boats don't, to be sure, speak in words; instead, they speak in noises. If you muscle your oars, for example, there will be a *thunk* noise on every stroke, as the button of your oar reunites with your oarlock. But this is only one noise in the rowing vocabulary.

If you drag your oars during the recovery, your blades will make a hissing noise. It is pretty much the same sound, I tell my athletes, as an audience of skilled rowers would make if they wanted to express their disapproval at oars being dragged. Row a bit cleaner than this, so that your oars touch the water intermittently during the recovery, and the hissing will be replaced by a disapproving *tsk-tsk* noise. If there is a gentle breeze, the blades will make a grinding noise as they encounter the ripples on the water. If the breeze picks up and those ripples turn into wavelets, the grinding will become a *tat-tat* noise. And if the wind picks up still more, the *tat-tat* will be replaced by the *whap* noise of blades slapping waves.

If you splash at the catch, the splash will make a *tchik* noise, kind of like a high-hat cymbal makes. And if you fail to fully plant a blade at the catch before putting pressure on it, it will make a distinctive *kerplunk* noise.

During the drive, if your blade is much too shallow, it will make a tearing noise in the water. If a blade is deeper than this but still too shallow, it will instead make a gurgling noise, as water flows over the top of the blade to fill in the air pocket that has formed behind it. If this gurgling noise starts late in the drive, it is because, although your blade is adequately deep early on, it rises as you approach the release.

If you pull your blade out of the water before you have finished the drive, it will sound like a bucket of water being thrown into a swimming pool, and with very good reason: make this mistake and you *will be* throwing water into water, only you will be using your oar blades rather than a bucket to throw it. Of all the noises caused by rowing mistakes, this is the loudest; in a bad case, it can be heard from a hundred meters away.

But this is just the beginning of the information with which your ears will provide you, if you know how to use them. They will, for example, help you find asymmetries in your rowing. If you are rowing in a symmetrical fashion, you will be treated to stereophonic sound: what you hear on the left side of the boat will be the same as what you hear on the right. If you hear different sounds, it is because you are doing different things with your left hand than you are with your right.

A rower can, with practice, learn how to "row with his ears": he can hear a certain noise, know what mistake he is making, and then correct that mistake, all without taking his eyes off his focal point on the horizon. If, for example, he hears a *tchik* noise on the left at the catch, he will lower his left hand a bit at the end of the recovery. This will get his blade up off the water so that the catch will be clean. If he hears a *thunk* noise on the right after the catch, he will relax his right arm. This will prevent him from pulling his oar away from the oarlock at the end of the recovery. His ears will also tell him when he has successfully dealt with whatever mistake he heard: the boat will stop making the symptomatic sound.

Even a well-rowed boat will make *some* sound. There will inevitably be the sound the bow makes slicing through the water. At the catch, there will be the *click* noise the rotated oar makes when the flat spot on the collar finds the flat spot on the oarlock. At the release, there will be another *click* noise, and maybe a *shush* noise as well, when the blades come out of the water. This last noise, by the way, is quite like the sound a strict librarian would make as a reminder to patrons to keep the noise down. Other than that, though, the boat will be remarkably quiet. And it isn't an accident that a well-rowed boat won't make much noise. Sound, as Charlie used to tell me, is wasted energy, and in a well-rowed boat, there will be very little wasted energy.

Most rowers, I have found, are oblivious to the sounds connected with rowing. Stated bluntly, they row deaf. Rather than trying intently to hear and diagnose the sounds the boat makes, they seem to tune out the various hisses, tchiks, and thunks to which their rowing gives rise. My theory is that they have, in their time as a rower, been desensitized to noise by being exposed to too much of it.

If the boats you row are invariably noisy, you learn to tune out the sounds of rowing, the way someone who lives next to a freeway stops hearing the whooshing sound made by passing cars, or the way someone who lives near an airport stops hearing the scream of the incoming jets. In the case of rowing, though, this selective deafness is unfortunate, since by ignoring the sounds of rowing, a rower is failing to make use of one of the most important self-diagnostic tools the sport has to offer.

Learn to "row with your ears," and every time you row, you will take along with you a very knowledgeable and attentive coach—namely, the boat itself. This "nautical coach" will never fail to show up for a workout. He will never turn his back on you or leave you to check on the progress of other rowers. Rather, he will monitor *your every stroke*, and without hesitation will tell you what you are doing wrong. And he won't just give you summaries of what you are doing wrong; he will tell you each and every time you do it. Indeed, he will provide real-time feedback: at *the very instant* you start doing something wrong, he will let you know.

The only drawback to this coach is that he doesn't speak English. Rather, he uses the various noises I have described. Thus, to benefit from his coaching, you will need to learn his language. Another thing to realize is that if you like praise, this coach leaves something to be desired. Row without making any major mistakes, and you won't hear words of congratulation. Instead, you will be rewarded with icy silence. This might be unsettling at first, but as you gain expertise in rowing with your ears, you will come to think of the sounds of silence as the sweetest praise there is in rowing. That the gods of rowing would provide us, free of charge, with this sort of built-in coach is another piece of evidence that they love us and want us to row well.

DESENSITIZATION DRILLS

But I have digressed. Let us turn our attention back to the ways in which a rower can desensitize himself to the fear of flipping. I have described the tap-at-hands-away drill. A rower who starts doing this drill can set numerical targets for himself. At first, the target might be to do five taps without stopping (and keep the boat balanced all the while). If he finds that he is tipping in one direction while tapping, he should stop to analyze what is causing him to do so. There must be some asymmetry in his posture. Otherwise, the boat would remain level.

Once the rower feels comfortable doing five taps, he can raise his target to ten and then twenty. (He might practice this drill over a period of several days, each day increasing his target number.) By the time a rower reaches twenty taps, he will likely have reached the stage at which he could tap all day long, if it weren't so boring to do so. He might thereby succeed in convincing his subconscious mind that a boat isn't a spiteful creature that will lurch one way or another for no good reason. Hopefully, his subconscious mind will then conclude that it has better things to worry about than malicious acts on the part of a boat.

When a rower is comfortable doing the tap-at-hands-away drill, there is an experiment he can do to discover just how important a role his eyes play in keeping his boat balanced. He can start out doing the drill with his eyes focused on the horizon, and then, when the boat is nicely balanced and the oars are bobbing away, he can try darting his eyes around on the horizon, try looking at the water instead of the horizon, try looking at his bobbing blades, or—the ultimate experiment—try closing his eyes. Unless he has exceptionally good balance, he will quickly come to appreciate how important it is to maintain visual focus while in a boat.

And if visual focus is important, so is mental focus. I have found that even though I continue to stare fixedly at my focal point, I can mess up a tap-at-hands-away drill merely by thinking about what is behind my back or thinking about my left blade bobbing in and out of the water. Sometimes, when I am teaching my athletes this drill, their boat will suddenly lurch in one direction, and they will have to feather their oars to stop from flipping. At that point, I might teasingly accuse them of ruining the set of their boat by having had an impure thought.

It isn't just during drills that mental focus is important. I have been in the middle of a race, rowing along nicely and, coming into the catch, have complimented myself on how well I was setting the boat. On more than one occasion, having this thought, at this moment, has caused my boat to lurch to one side. It is as if the gods of rowing detected my hubris and decided to put me in my place.

This is why I tell novice rowers that it is important that as they row, they keep their mind on their rowing. Indeed, not only should they concentrate on rowing in general, but they should focus their attention on *the very stroke they are in the midst of*. Start having thoughts about their next stroke, and there is a good chance that they will sabotage the current one. Many a crab has been caught in this way.

The tap-at-hands-away drill, besides helping a rower overcome his fear of flipping and teaching him to stay visually and mentally focused, has a beneficial side-effect: doing this drill will likely improve his posture. The rower will find out what it means to sit upright in the boat, which will make it easier for him to set the boat, which in turn will make it less likely that he will do something that will cause the boat to flip.

When you have mastered the tap-at-hands-away drill, you can move on to a more challenging tap drill, called *tap at the catch*. To do this drill, you move—again, in a stationary boat—to the catch position. Your seat will be all the way toward the stern, far enough so that your shins are vertical (but not beyond vertical). You then lean forward at the waist and reach out with your arms, with your blades still feathered. Now, stare at your focal point, square your blades, and start bobbing them in and out of the water.

Lots of rowers will find this drill to be not just challenging but too challenging. Just sitting at the catch will make them nervous, and when they start tapping their oars and their boat gets tippy, they will panic, feather their oars, and slide back in their seats. They might, thereafter, refuse to attempt this drill.

These rowers might want to try the *sliding-tap drill*, which is a hybrid of the above two tap drills. To do this drill, you start out by doing the tap-at-hands-away drill: you bob your oars into and out of the water while sitting at hands-away. When you feel comfortable doing this, you start slowly moving down the slide, bobbing all the while. You move as far down the slide as your courage will allow, and then you start slowly sliding back toward the bow, still bobbing. Practice this enough, and you will someday be able to go all the way to the catch and tap there to your heart's content. At that point, you will be ready to attempt the more demanding tap-at-the-catch drill, in which you move to the catch position *before* you start tapping.

The tap-at-hands-away drill can help you develop good posture at the release. The sliding-tap drill, by way of contrast, can help you develop good posture during the recovery. By tapping as you slide toward the stern, you can discover the exact point at which you lose your balance. You can then think about the asymmetry that surely must be coming into existence at that point. Does a knee start sticking out? Does your torso start to twist? Do you start doing something different with your hands? (If your hands break horizontal symmetry during the recovery—if, in particular, your left hand "leads" your right—it can affect boat set.) Find the asymmetry, and you can eliminate it, thereby taking one more important step toward developing your ability to set the boat.

It can be frustrating for rowers to attempt the tap drills described above: the boat just won't balance, meaning that maybe they just don't have it in them to balance a boat. To such rowers, I can offer these words of encouragement: in the act of carrying their boat to the dock so they could go out and practice tap drills, they performed a feat of balance that in theory is far more difficult than the balance required by the drills: they were not only standing upright, but walking while carrying an unwieldy burden. In other words, their ability to balance on dry land is overwhelming evidence that their body's balance mechanism is fully functional. They just need to learn how to put that mechanism to work in a boat.

For someone with a fear of flipping, tapping at the catch is therapeutic because it forces her to spend time doing the thing that scares her. Another way to accomplish this is by doing a drill that I call *rowing the catch*. To do this drill, you catch water as usual, but instead of pulling all the way through the drive, you stop when your slide is maybe halfway back (your knees will still be bent), release your oars, and then go back to the catch. In this drill, your recovery will be quite short, and as a result, your stroke rate will be high.

Rowing the catch forces you to spend time in the tippiest part of the stroke. When you first try this drill, you can cheat a bit and not slide all the way bow-ward at the catch; you can stop, in other words, before your shins are vertical. But as you do the drill and thereby develop confidence at the catch, you should experiment with sliding farther sternward and reaching out more with your hands. If you spend some time doing this drill, you will find, when you return to regular rowing, that the catch doesn't seem that scary any more.

ACKNOWLEDGING OUR FEARS

Although lots of rowers have a fear of flipping, many are unwilling to admit as much. And even those who admit it might not be cognizant of the extent to which that fear distorts their rowing technique. What this means is that when rowers approach you for help with their rowing, they almost never say, "I have a fear of flipping. Can you help me overcome it so that I can row better?" Instead, they will tell you about a specific rowing problem that is vexing them: "I splash at the catch; can you help me stop splashing?"

When I encounter such a rower, I might go out with her in a double, with me sitting at bow. As soon as I, quite predictably, get splashed, I tell her that all she needs to do to cure her splashing problem is to lower her hands by an inch or two going into the catch. If this fixes the problem, the patient is cured. Usually, though, this does not fix the problem. The rower continues to splash, and I respond by bringing the boat to a halt and talking to her about her fear of flipping and the steps she can take to overcome that fear.

Rowers are sometimes puzzled by this response. They assume that I haven't been listening to what they have been saying and try to get me back on topic: "Actually, my problem isn't a fear of flipping; it is splashing at the catch. I need to know what to do to stop splashing." On hearing this, I will point out that I *just told them* how to stop splashing: they need only lower their hands going into the catch. The fact that they were unable to do something that should be physically quite easy to do is pretty compelling evidence that their problem is psychological in nature. More precisely, they have a fear of flipping. Overcome this fear, and they will find it easy to lower their hands at the catch, and their splashing will be a thing of the past.

In many cases, rowers reject the notion that their rowing ability is circumscribed by fear; indeed, to prove how brave they are, they might offer to flip a boat while I watch. The fear I am talking about, though, is not the kind that makes you tremble; it is instead an anxiety that distorts your rowing. Golfers experience a similar phenomenon. When a golfer has what are called "the yips," his anxiety about missing putts distorts his swing in a way that causes him to miss putts. Likewise, when a rower has what I call *flipophobia*, the anxiety she experiences during the recovery will cause her to row defensively, which in turn might mean that she drags her oars, rushes to a premature catch, or splashes at that catch.

Sometimes when I am coaching a rower who, despite displaying all the symptoms of flipophobia, denies experiencing anxiety during the recovery, I will stop describing her as being fearful and will instead tell her (after a brief discussion of golf) that she is suffering from the "nautical yips." It is terminology that most rowers find tolerable.

What rowers want, quite understandably, is a quick and easy cure for their rowing ailments. They want a bandage, not a body cast. Consequently, when I start talking about undertaking a program to overcome their fear of flipping (or their nautical yips), they become impatient. Such a program would require weeks or even months of effort on their part. They will insist that they need to spend that time getting ready for an upcoming regatta. They can't just sit around doing tap drills; they have to be doing sprints to build themselves up.

I tell these rowers that time spent dealing with their flipophobia will be time very well spent. Yes, the steps necessary to deal with their psychological issues might set back their training this regatta season, but it is an investment that will pay abundant dividends during the rest of their rowing career. I add that if they are serious about their rowing, it is a sacrifice they should be willing to make. Sometimes the rowers with whom I have this conversation believe me.

I should add that rowers aren't the only ones tempted by "bandage solutions" to rowing problems; coaches can be as well. A coach who offers what looks like a quick-and-easy solution to a difficult problem—"All you need to do is move your foot stretchers sternward by one notch"—will be giving the rower what he wants, and that rower will be thankful. The coach will also look brilliant for having known about this solution. And who knows, the bandage might even work for a while: the placebo effect can be as powerful in rowing as it is in medicine.

In the long run, though, learning to row well requires patience on the part of a rower. Rely on bandage solutions to rowing problems, and before long you will look like a mummy. Your rowing ability will plateau at an unnecessarily low level.

To be sure, there are rowing problems that have quick and easy solutions. I am simply arguing that there is a cluster of common problems—dragged oars during the recovery, a rushed recovery, a premature catch, and a splash at the catch—that are quite likely the result of a fear of flipping, and that until this fear is overcome, these problems are unlikely to go away.

A CONFESSION

Let me end my discussion of flipophobia by describing my own experience with it. In my first few years of rowing—before Charlie took me under his wing—my rowing was dominated by a fear of flipping. As a result, I had all the fear-related symptoms I have described. Because I was clutching my oars, the palms of my hands developed horrible blisters that subsequently became hideous calluses. I routinely dragged my oars and had, as I have said, the worst and most consistent splashes at the catch that I have ever seen. (Indeed, quite possibly it was the worst splash in the history of the world, but I don't want to seem boastful in the claims I make regarding it.) Other rowers would tell me to lower my hands in order to get my blades up off the water. My brain would issue a command to that effect, but my arms would not obey.

Even now, I do not regard myself as someone who has vanquished his fear of flipping; rather, I am a recovering flipophobic. There are occasions when the old fears come back, and when they do, my old habits reemerge, and my rowing becomes defensive.

One of these occasions is when, in early spring, I take a single out after having been off the water for three months. I am invariably surprised by how tremulous the boat is. I push off from the dock and quickly start wondering what I've let myself in for.

Another occasion is when I take a novice rower out in a double on a coached row. The novice will be randomly catching crabs, and as a result, the boat will be lurching from side to side. If the novice in question is, say, six inches taller than me and sixty pounds heavier, the resulting row will be the nautical equivalent of an amusement park ride. I find myself dragging my blades. I also start clutching my oar handles and might, by the end of the row, discover new blisters on my palms and fingers, as well as gashes on the back of my right hand. In this case, though, someone could argue that what I am experiencing is not flip-ophobia but a completely rational response to a clear-and-present danger of flipping.

One other time when I can feel the fear of flipping is when I am racing in difficult conditions—when I am, for example, rowing in choppy water or in a wind that gusts from the side. I become anxious and start rowing defensively. I drag my oars and shorten my drive. Perhaps this is once again the sensible thing for me to be doing under the circumstances in which I find myself. All I can say, though, is that in my case, the defensive rowing isn't a consciously adopted strategy; to the contrary, I cannot help but do it. The rowers who beat me on these occasions do not likewise seem compelled to resort to defensive rowing. I wish I had their confidence.

The water on which I practice is on a sheltered stretch of river. As a result, I row on a lot of flat water, and in the summer, on water that is glassy. It is great for rowing, but it is not so good for someone who wants to elicit his fear of flipping so he can practice dealing with that fear. I respond to this situation by going out of my way to find bad water in which to row. When I see the wake left by a coaching launch—a wake that will make the boat rock in a precarious manner—I make a point of rowing through it rather than bracing for it with feathered oars. On windy days, I find the windiest part of the course and row back and forth there, trying my best to keep my blades up off the water and reach far at the catch. On these days, I also like to do a version of the tap-at-hands-away drill that I call the *sideways-tap drill*: I turn my boat sideways to the oncoming waves and start tapping at hands away. This will cause the boat to start rocking from side to side, which all by itself will make me feel ill at ease. It is wonderfully therapeutic.

I have discovered that how active my fear of flipping is depends on what size boat I am in: the bigger the boat is, the more confident I am of my rowing. Put me in a quad, and I can easily row clean and reach way out of the boat at the catch. A quad is, after all, a very stable platform for rowing. In a double, I am a bit less confident than this but still far more confident than I am in a single.

This means that if I plan to race a single, I need to resist the temptation to train in bigger boats. The more time I spend in a single, the more confident I will feel rowing one.

SIX

Getting Set

The tap and glide drills I have described are quite useful for *finding* stroke asymmetries. The question then becomes, how best to *eliminate* them? In response to this question, allow me to describe some drills that force rowers to repeatedly encounter their asymmetries so they can work on them—more precisely, so they can embed a new way of rowing into their muscle memory. If they can accomplish this, their "default" manner of rowing will be to row symmetrically, and they will find themselves "automatically" rowing with set.

The first drills I will describe are *pause drills*. Unlike the tap drills I described earlier, pause drills are done in a moving boat. To do a pause drill, you get your boat to cruising speed and then pause at some point in your stroke. So far, this sounds like the glide drills—glide-at-hands-away and glide-at-the-catch—I have described, but in those drills, after you pause, you let the boat glide until you have tipped one way or the other and the drag of your blades on the water brings the boat to a stop. In pause drills, by way of contrast, you pause only until the boat starts feeling tippy, and then you start rowing again. After taking a few strokes to bring the boat back up to speed, you again pause. By doing pause drills, you end up spending more of your workout time balancing the boat than you would by doing glide drills.

In the *pause-at-hands-away drill*, you stop rowing when your hands are past your knees during the recovery. You pause there for a time, *with your blades off the water*, and then continue rowing. In one standard form of this drill, you might take three strokes, pause, and then take another three strokes.

If this drill seems too easy, you can switch to the *pause-at-the-catch* drill. In this drill, you pause not at hands-away, but at the catch, after you have moved all the way to the stern-end of the slide. You sit there with your blades feathered above the water. How long you pause there depends on how confident of your set you are. It might be for a few tenths of a second or might be for a second or more. When the pause ends, you square your blades, catch water, and continue rowing.

There are variations of this drill that are even more demanding. You can pause at the catch with your blades squared instead of feathered. (If you try this drill, keep in mind that if your squared blades touch the water while you are gliding at the catch, you will probably go for a swim.) And for the daredevil rower, there is a variation of pause-at-the-catch that is more demanding still. After pausing at the catch, you "wash your handles" before starting to row again: you literally dip the butts of your oar handles into the water. (This drill is best done in a boat with sternward-pointing "wing" riggers.) Yes, your blades will be sticking way up in the air when you do this. And yes, you will have to be reaching way forward in the boat to be able to dip your handles. But it *can* be done. Not by me, though.

SLOW ROWING

Other worthwhile set drills involve rowing slowly. In the first such drill, you row at regular power but at a slow stroke rate. The key thing in doing this drill is to concentrate on keeping your blades up off the water during the recovery and not letting them splash at the catch. You might initially do this drill at 18 strokes per minute. Many rowers with set problems find it difficult to do this, for the simple reason that they have trouble balancing the boat during the recovery. This drill forces them to spend lots of time (more than two seconds per stroke, in fact) practicing balancing the boat.

When a rower becomes comfortable rowing at 18 strokes per minute, the target stroke rate can be lowered. Do this drill (eventually) at 12 strokes per minute, and you will be taking a stroke every 5 seconds, meaning that you will be in recovery mode, with your oars off the water, for more than 4 seconds every stroke.

Let me pause here to address the merits of rowing with a metronome. In my workouts, I sometimes use a small digital metronome. It was intended for use by musicians, but I find that it is quite useful in the slow-stroke-rate drills I have been describing. I can't set my metronome to give me 12 beats a minute; musicians apparently never have a need to play this slowly. I can set it, though, to give me 36 beats a minute in a waltz-like ONE-two-three rhythm, with the ONE beat sounding different from the other two. To row at 12 strokes per minute, I simply catch water on every ONE beat.

Using a metronome in this manner lets me row at a slow stroke rate for extended periods without having to look at a digital stroke-rate monitor, an action that could affect the set of my boat. If I want to practice a higher stroke rate than 12, I need only turn up the tempo: 54 beats per minute, for example, would give me 18 ONE beats per minute, for a stroke rate of 18.

Another drill that can help rowers learn to set a boat is what I call *slow-motion-rowing*. To "slo-mo-row," you row at a normal stroke rate but apply very little power. (Thus, it won't be your *stroke-rate* that is slow; it will be your *boat*.) During the recovery, you hold your blades high off the water. And the key thing is that when you go into the catch and feel your level of anxiety rising, you try to control yourself. You don't let the boat tell you when to catch, and you certainly don't let your fear tell you when to catch; *you* decide when you are going to catch. Rather than rushing to the catch, you might even decelerate coming up to it. As a result, your catch will look leisurely.

If the boat starts to tip, you have the option of catching prematurely. But having done so, you need to redouble your effort, on the next stroke, not to let it happen again. By doing this, you can develop your ability to row *with authority*. Your goal here is to teach the boat who is in charge: it will not be able to dictate to you when you catch water; to the contrary, you will catch when you are good and ready to catch.

If you spend, say, half-an-hour doing these slow-stroke-rate or slow-motion-rowing drills, and then start rowing at a regular stroke rate and regular power, you might find that you are rowing quite cleanly, in large part because you are successfully balancing your boat. What has happened is that because you increased your stroke rate, you have less time to spend during the recovery—meaning less time for the boat to be in the tippy part of the stroke. And more important, the time you spent rowing slow will have forced you to row symmetrically, and this symmetrical rowing will still be in your muscle memory when you start rowing fast. The general principle: if you can row clean at 20 strokes per minute, you can row very clean at 28.

You can also combine slo-mo-rowing with regular rowing to explore the limits of your rowing form. You can, for example, do ten strokes "on" (meaning pulling hard) and ten strokes "off." During the ten "off" strokes, you revert to slo-mo-rowing. During that time, you will just be going through the motions of rowing, but doing so cleanly and with authority. Then, when you apply power during your ten "on" strokes, you try to retain as much of that good form and authority as you can.

You will probably find that your form deteriorates during the ten "on" strokes. This is because the application of power amplifies the impact your rowing asymmetries have on boat set. At low power, for example, you might be able to get away with rowing with one oar deeper than the other during the drive. Increase the power, though, and the boat will start rocking. This rocking will in turn make it harder for you to release your blades cleanly and to catch water without splashing. Your blades will soon be hacking at the water, and your rowing efficiency will plummet.

Sometimes in my coaching, I encounter a very strong person who has decided to take up rowing. This individual might be magnificent on a rowing machine—on which set is never an issue. But because he lacks technique, he cannot effectively transmit the power at his disposal into the blades of his oars, where it can propel the boat. Instead, the power gets wasted making the boat rock. This rocking causes the rower to catch crabs, which in turn causes the boat to slow down. In response to this situation, he is likely to start applying even more power—another example of a counter-solution—only to have the boat respond by slowing down even more. How frustrating!

The biggest challenge in coaching such a rower is to make him realize that although the application of raw power might solve the problems that arise in many sports, this approach simply won't work in a form-intensive sport like rowing. Indeed, his big challenge will be to restrain the power at his disposal until he has learned proper form. Only then will his power be an asset in the boat. Until that time, he is the rowing equivalent of a muscle car with a 400-horsepower engine but a defective transmission.

The ten-on, ten-off drill is custom-made for powerful rowers. I like to take them out in a double specifically to do this drill. We start out at very low power. On each "on" segment, we increase the power a bit until the rower's form breaks. When it does, we try to figure out the asymmetry that caused it to break. On the next set of "on" strokes, we back off the power a bit. In other words, we spend our time pushing the envelope of the rower's ability to effectively apply power, with the goal of eventually reaching the point at which he can maintain form while applying full power—the way, I like to remind rowers, that Olympians do.

I encourage rowers to do this drill in a single, in which the asymmetries in their rowing will become more obvious. I also remind them that their goal during the ten off strokes, during which they are rowing with very little power, is to row not fast but perfectly, and that when they up the power for their "on" strokes, their goal is to retain as much of this perfect form as they can.

This drill has variations. Obviously, it can be done with more than ten "on" and "off" strokes. Also, the "on" strokes, instead of being "hard" strokes (with higher power but a normal stroke rate) can be "high" strokes (with normal power but a higher stroke rate). We have seen that increasing the power you apply can affect your form, but so can raising the stroke rate. The higher the stroke rate is, the less time you have to get things done on each stroke. In particular, your release becomes more challenging, and you might find yourself catching crabs that you wouldn't otherwise have caught. Thus, raising your stroke rate is a wonderful way to see how robust your release is and to improve the precision of that release.

SEEKING PERFECTION

After you have made progress in discovering and overcoming the asymmetries in your rowing and thereby made progress in gaining the ability to set a boat, there is one other drill you can do. I call it the *perfection drill*, and it is easy to explain: see how many strokes you can take before you have one that is imperfect. You might, on that stroke, catch a crab. Less dramatically, you might touch an oar to the water during the recovery, splash a bit at the catch, or have a less-than-clean release.

It is easy to detect *constant* flaws in rowing form. It is also fairly easy, if you are observant and diligent, to overcome them. After all, they are always there for you to work on. It is rather more challenging, however, to detect and deal with *sporadic* flaws. (In much the same way, a car with an intermittent short in its electrical system will be harder to diagnose than a car whose electrical system is flat out dead.) That is the motivation for doing the perfection drill. You row until a sporadic flaw reveals itself.

The defective stroke, when it finally comes, represents a teachable moment. The rower needs to do a post-mortem on that stroke. What went wrong? And in asking this question, he should be interested not only in *what the mistake was* (such as that he caught a crab) but in *why he made that mistake* (perhaps he "looked ahead" at the moment of the catch, and thereby threw the boat off balance). He also should keep in mind that what caused his form to blow up on, say, stroke number seventeen might have been something that happened one or more strokes earlier: it was in those strokes that he lit the fuse of the bomb that finally detonated on stroke seventeen. (If you are averse to the analysis of long causal chains, rowing is not the sport for you.) By doing this sort of detective work, a rower can start eliminating the sporadic flaws in his rowing technique and thereby, perhaps, take his rowing ability to the next level.

The perfection drill can be done at any stroke rate, but important lessons can be learned from doing it at both very low stroke rates (it will reveal your set issues) and uncomfortably high stroke rates (it will reveal your timing issues). Also, if you can do this drill in relatively flat water, in which your boat leaves a long visible wake, the drill will reveal subtle imperfections in your rowing form. You might think that you just did ten perfect strokes, but if you look back and see that your wake was less than perfectly straight, you have compelling evidence that your rowing was less than perfectly symmetrical during those strokes. The imperfections in question were so small that they were not apparent in any one stroke, but their cumulative impact was readily visible.

One last thought on perfection: to have a chance in the Olympics, you have to be able to do more than two-hundred perfect strokes—and do them at full power.

BECOMING ONE WITH THE BOAT

I have now described several things a rower can do to gain the ability to set a boat. All involve conscious effort. Here, though, is the final key to setting a boat: stop trying to set it! You should, in other words, take a Zen-like approach to setting a boat. Allow me to explain.

Zen Buddhists tell us that if we are to have a good life, we must overcome desire. They add that it is impossible to overcome desire by consciously trying to overcome it, since our trying will only create one more desire for us to overcome. So how are we to overcome desire? By gaining enlightenment—and they will quickly add that you can't gain enlightenment by trying to gain enlightenment. To the contrary, the best way to gain enlightenment is to adopt a certain lifestyle and do certain Zen exercises. Then the day will come when you experience your moment of enlightenment—maybe. In Zen, there are no guaranteed outcomes.

The same thing happens in learning to set a boat. The worst way to learn to set a boat is by consciously trying to balance it. Instead, your efforts should be spent consciously trying to remove the asymmetries in your stroke. Then, with luck, the day will come when you are out rowing—utterly relaxed, thinking about nothing in particular—and you realize, to your astonishment, that your boat is setting itself! You will have achieved the rowing equivalent of enlightenment.

Don't get me wrong. Rowers *should* spend time rowing thoughtfully. They should observe themselves as they row, and on the basis of their observations, they should critique themselves. But the goal of thoughtful rowing is so they can row without thinking—so they can, as Charlie used to put it, "just row."

The idea is that by doing lots of thoughtful rowing, you will teach your body what correct rowing feels like. Correct rowing, as I've explained, involves some very unnatural motions, but if you do these motions enough, they get embedded into your muscle memory and start feeling natural. When this happens, you will be able, when you row, to put yourself onto the biological equivalent of autopilot.

You will find yourself in a heightened state of awareness as you move along. Three of your five senses will be fully engaged: you will be staring at your focal point on the horizon, you will be feeling the resistance of the oars in your hands and the levelness of the boat beneath you, and you will be listening carefully to the sounds your blades are making. You will make slight form adjustments based on the reports of your senses. You will, as they say, become one with your boat. You will be so fully engaged in your rowing that the rest of the world will drop away.

I have had this happen. Not as often as I would like it to, though.

Part Two

The Stroke

SEVEN

The Catch

In part one of this book, I undertook a lengthy and I think essential discussion of symmetry, set, and fear. I also explained the importance of caring about and even obsessing about technique if one is to row well. In part two, I turn my attention to a detailed examination of rowing technique. In this examination, I will move through the components of a stroke—the catch, drive, release, and recovery—and talk about what should and shouldn't be happening during each component, and why these things should or shouldn't be happening.

Before I begin this examination, though, some clarification is in order. The rowing stroke is usually said to have four components, and the standard order in which to list these components is as follows: the *catch*, when the squared oar blades are lowered into the water; the *drive*, when the oar handles are pulled to propel the boat; the *release*, when the blades are removed from the water and feathered; and the *recovery*, when the blades are moved back to the catch. There are two problems with this list.

To begin with, the choice of which component should come first is utterly arbitrary. It makes just as much sense to start the list with, say, the release as it does to start with the catch. A rowing stroke is, after all, a profoundly circular event. It is true that the power is delivered to the water during the drive, and this delivery of power is what rowing is about. But without a catch, the drive wouldn't be possible. And without a recovery, the catch would happen at the same point as the release, and the drive length would be zero.

So picking the "beginning" of a stroke is like trying to tell which season begins the year. Should the list begin with spring? Why not winter? And if you argue that winter is the first season since it is what season it is during January, the month that begins the year, I will reply that winter officially begins not in January but in December, the last month of the year, meaning that winter should be the last season of the year; and if this isn't enough to convince you that you are mistaken, I will add that it is utterly arbitrary that calendar years begin in January instead of, say, October.

The second problem with the above listing of the component parts of a stroke is that it is not clear when one component has ended and the next has begun. Rather, the components tend to blend into each other.

Consider the release. Obviously, this component will include the interval during which the hands are pushed down to release the blade from the water—hence, the name *release*—but where will this component end? Some people argue that as soon as the blade is out of the water, the release has ended and the recovery has begun. Other people point out that, after releasing the blades, the rower should keep moving his hands to the "hands away" position; to do otherwise is to commit the technical blunder known as "pausing at the release." These people therefore argue that the release isn't over until the rower's hands are at "hands away."

Or consider the dividing line between the catch and the drive. It might be argued that the catch ends when the blades are fully submerged in the water and that the drive begins when the rower starts pulling on the oar handles to drive those blades sternward. As we shall see in chapter 8, though, the rower must start pulling on the handles to move the blades sternward *while they are still descending*. Otherwise, the blades won't be stationary with respect to the water they are entering, and a splash will be kicked up as a result.

So is "hands away" part of the release or part of the recovery? And when does the drive *really* begin? How you answer these questions is somewhat arbitrary. They are therefore topics well-suited for debate among rowers who find themselves, because of a sudden summer thunderstorm, confined to the boathouse and in desperate need of something to do.

THE GREAT ROLL-UP DEBATE

I will (arbitrarily) begin my discussion of the stroke with the catch. The catch sounds as easy as pie: at the end of the recovery, you square your blades and drop them into the water. The problem is that the catch is when, as I have explained, your boat is at its tippiest, meaning that something that should be easy is in fact tricky.

Preparation for the catch begins when the rower starts to rotate his hands to square his blades. There are two theories on when to do this. The first recommends what is called an *early roll-up*: maybe as early as halfway through the recovery, you start slowly rotating your blades, with the goal of achieving full squareness just before it is time to catch. The other theory recommends that you wait to square your blades until very late in the recovery, just before you submerge them. We might call this a *late roll-up*, although some refer to it—disparagingly, I have always thought—as a *flip catch*. It is important to note that in both sorts of catches, you move down the slide at the same rate. The difference is in when, as you move down the slide, you start rotating your hands.

These two kinds of roll-ups not only look different but sound different. A late roll-up will cause an audible click as the oars switch quickly from one stable position (with the flat surface of the oar collar pressed against the flat surface of the oarlock) to the other stable position. With an early roll-up, this noise will be missing or at least much subdued.

I am an advocate of late roll-ups.* I agree that an early roll-up might look prettier and more graceful than a late one, but competitive rowing is not a beauty pageant. It is all about moving a boat fast. And this means that an early roll-up has a serious drawback: the blade of a rolled-up oar creates "sail area," which in turn gives rise to wind resistance. Since wind resistance is a bad thing, the longer you can keep your blade feathered, the better. This, in a nutshell, is the argument for a late roll-up.

When considering the problem of blade wind-resistance, it is important to realize that the blades are exposed to a stronger headwind than any other part of the boat. Suppose that a rower is rowing at 8 mph in air that is calm (with respect to the water). He will experience an 8-mph headwind. But during the recovery, his blades will be moving toward the bow with respect to him. This means that they will be experiencing a headwind of about 15 miles per hour.†

---

*There is also, I am told, a roll-up debate in sweep rowing, but since I am a sculler, I will not offer an opinion on that debate.

†If an oar with 2 meters of outboard sweeps through 90 degrees during the recovery, its arc will be a bit more than 3 meters long. If the recovery takes 1.5 seconds, it will be traveling (relative to the boat) at 2 meters per second, or nearly 5 miles per hour. Add 5-mph of blade speed to 8-mph of boat speed, and you get 13-mph of wind on the blades of the oars. Elite rowers, though, probably have a sweep

How big a deal is a 15-mph breeze on the blades? To find out, there is an experiment you can do. The next time it is windy—ideally, the next time the wind is blowing at 15 mph—take two oars outside and hold them vertically in the wind, like flagpoles. Rotate one so its blade is feathered with respect to the wind and rotate the other so its blade is square to the wind. There will be a significant difference in how hard the wind pushes the two oars.

Realize, though, that 15 mph is the relevant number if you are rowing a boat *in calm air*. If you are instead rowing into a headwind, the wind resistance caused by an early roll-up will be even worse. Thus, row a boat at 8 mph into a 20-mph headwind, and because of the motion of your blades relative to the boat, your blades will feel a 35-mph headwind. Good luck getting them up to the catch! (Indeed, even if you feather your oars, the wind resistance presented by the oar *shafts* under these circumstances will make it interestingly difficult to move the oars to the catch.)

Above, I have referred to the "sail area" of oar blades, but it would have been more accurate to refer to their "parachute area." Sails, after all, move things forward; parachutes slow things down. It is hard enough to move a boat through the water. It is harder still to move it with parachutes attached to the ends of your oars. But this is precisely what you are doing if you square your oars sooner than you have to—if, in other words, you have an early roll-up.

The wind resistance caused by an early roll-up can have a significant impact on boat performance. Indeed, according to one estimate, rolling your blades up 10 degrees (of oar sweep) earlier than you have to will, in calm air, cost you 1.5 seconds in a 2000-meter race. Row that race in an 11-mile-per-hour headwind, though, and this early roll-up will cost you 3 seconds.* In elite competition, this cost would be huge.

Having said this, I should add that elite rowers are forced to have what *looks like* an early rollup. This is because how many degrees of roll-up a rower has depends on her stroke rate. Re-

---

of greater than 90 degrees and almost certainly have a recovery time shorter than 1.5 seconds, meaning that their blades will be moving even faster relative to the boat. Their boats will also be moving faster than 8 mph. Thus, the faster you are, the more reason there is to delay squaring your blade for the catch.

Rowing Biomechanics Newsletter (April, 2006).

search by Dr. Valery Kleshnev,* for example, shows that a rower who starts rolling up 15 degrees before the catch when she is rowing at 20 strokes per minute might start rolling up 40 degrees before the catch when she is rowing at 37 strokes per minute, as might be necessary in elite competition. It isn't that the rower is consciously rolling up early; it's that the high stroke rate means that her oars are moving much faster, which in turn means that even though she spends *the same amount of time* rolling up at a stroke rate of 37 as she did at a rate of 20, her oars will have covered *a substantially bigger angle*. Bottom line: although a rower should not go out of her way to roll up earlier than necessary, if she rows at a high stroke rate, it will look like she is doing this.

It is, by the way, unfortunate that higher stroke rates translate into bigger roll-up angles in this manner. A higher stroke rate, after all, means (up to a point), a faster boat, which in turn magnifies the wind-resistance problems caused by an early roll-up. Ideally, a competitive rower would keep her roll-up angle constant: she would square her oars faster and faster as her stroke rate went up, thereby maintaining, say, 15 degrees of roll-up angle. But if you have ever tried rowing 37 strokes per minute for 2000 meters, you will realize that this is a lot to ask.

Having made this case against early roll-ups, I should add that under *some* circumstances, an unnecessarily early roll-up can make sense. In particular, if someone is rowing in a strong tailwind, the wind resistance provided by squared blades can be beneficial to the forward motion of the boat. They will, for once, act as sails, not parachutes. Indeed, I met a rower who told me that during a sprint race, in which the tailwind was particularly brisk, she did the most extreme early roll-up possible: she didn't feather her oars at all. She simply kept them square throughout the recovery. Doing this, she said, gave her an easy victory.

Besides the wind resistance issues raised by an early roll-up, there is a water resistance issue. If there are any waves—and in particular, if waves are irregular in height—it makes sense to keep your blades feathered as long as you can during the recovery. When a feathered blade encounters the top of a "rogue wave," it does a pretty good job of slicing through. When a squared or semi-squared blade encounters that same wave, it whacks it, thereby checking the forward motion of the boat and

---

*Rowing Biomechanics Newsletter (October, 2012).

disrupting the set of the boat as well. It might also knock the boat off course or, even worse, knock the oar out of the rower's hand.

A moment ago, I gave the argument for keeping the blades square during the recovery when rowing in a strong tailwind. But if that tailwind causes waves—as it almost always will—it makes sense to keep the blades feathered instead. This is because the benefits that can be derived from "sailing" in a tailwind will likely be more than offset by the harm done if your "sails" get hit by waves. In short, the conditions in which it might make sense to use a radically early roll-up will be pretty rare.

Those who favor an early roll-up might respond to the above comments by pointing out that during such a roll-up, the blades will come to square slowly, meaning that the wind resistance they offer won't be as bad as I have suggested. Nor will the water resistance. My response: while it is true that rowing with semi-deployed parachutes at the end of your oars is preferable to rowing with fully-deployed parachutes, why have any parachutes at all when it is possible to avoid them?

Another way someone might defend early roll-ups is by pointing out that they force you to keep your blades up off the water and thus prevent you from dragging them during the recovery, which would slow down your boat. Early roll-ups also lessen the chance that you will splash at the catch.

In response to this line of reasoning, I would point out that although an early roll-up may indeed help you overcome the problem of dragged oars and splashing at the catch, there is a much better way to accomplish this: just hold your hands an inch or so lower during the recovery. Do this, and your feathered blades won't drag on the water, and when you square them, there will be enough clearance between them and the water that you will be splash-free.

Early roll-ups are my candidate for the strangest thing that you hear otherwise-sensible scullers advocate. For early roll-ups to be defensible, there would have to be very good reasons for doing them—reasons good enough to top the wind-resistance and wave-collision reasons for not doing them. And yet, when you look for these reasons, they prove elusive.

This is a wonderful example, I think, of a case in which coaches repeat advice their coaches gave them, who in turn were repeating the advice *their* coaches gave *them*—and so on, back to the dawn of rowing history.* Some of the advice we inherit from our rowing ancestors is very good advice, such as the advice to use a sliding seat. But other advice, although bad, is not recognized as such because it is repeated so often. One assumes that "all these rowers" can't be mistaken. But if "all these rowers" are victims of groupthink—if they are all simply repeating things they have heard instead of analyzing carefully the things they hear—it is possible for them all to be very much mistaken.

If you are a rowing coach, it can be demoralizing to have your efforts undone by a single offhand remark made by a self-appointed coach. Suppose you work long and hard with a rower to overcome his catch problems. You go out in a double with him and quietly endure the splashing caused by his defective catch. You study his form so you can correct his asymmetries. And finally you are making real progress. Then you encounter this same rower out on the water, and he has an even worse catch than before you coached him. "What happened?" you ask.

"Bob saw me rowing and says I have a late roll-up," he replies, "so I've had to dramatically change the recovery you taught me. And oh, by the way, why didn't you mention my roll-up problem?"

Sigh! In the same way as too many cooks can spoil the broth, too many coaches can spoil a rower's form, particularly if those coaches do little more than repeat things they have heard.

CATCH DRILLS

But enough about the Great Roll-up Debate! Let us, for the sake of argument, assume that a rower uses the late roll-up I have advocated: she waits, that is, as long as possible during the recovery before squaring her blades. It is obviously important that this rower have her feathered blades up off the water when she finally squares them; otherwise, the bottom edge of the blades will chip the water, resulting in a splash.

As we have seen, there are two ways a rower, when she squares her blades at the catch, can cause a splash. The first and most obvious way is to drag her oars *throughout* the recovery.

---

*I haven't seen it with my own eyes, but I have heard that in Homer's *Odyssey*, in which there is a fair amount of rowing, Odysseus at one point mocks Eurylochus for having a flip catch.

The second, more interesting way is to keep her feathered blades up off the water through most of the recovery but then, as she is coming up to the catch, touch her feathered blades to the surface of the water. (This is what I referred to, back in chapter 4, as a *touch-and-go catch*.) Both these splashes, I have argued, are the result of a rower lacking confidence in the set of the boat, which in turn is likely a result of flipophobia.

Back in chapter 5, I described a drill that I called *rowing the catch*, in which a rower completes only the first part of the drive before releasing her oars and returning to the catch. Doing this drill can be doubly beneficial to someone with a splash problem. It gives her lots of catches to practice, and it forces her to spend time in the tippy part of the stroke, which will help her overcome the fears that emerge at that time, which in turn can help her overcome her splash problem.

There is, however, a second, less demanding drill that can help a rower work on a splash problem. This drill, which I call *rowing the release*, complements the row-the-catch drill. To row the release, you row with your arms and back only; your legs remain extended throughout the drill. To keep the boat moving during this drill, you will have to pick up your stroke rate. Thus, doing this drill will give you plenty of catches to work on. Not only that, but it will let you work on them when your boat is fairly stable. It is therefore a good initial drill for someone trying to overcome a splash problem.

Once a rower can "row the release" without splashing at the catch, she can modify this drill by involving the slide in her stroke. At first, she should go a quarter of the way down the slide, being careful to put her hands in the same position at the catch as they previously were. When she can do this without splashing, she can try moving halfway down the slide, and so on. She can thereby teach her hands what they have to do for her to become a splash-free rower.

In chapter 6, I described the pause-at-the-catch drill: you go to the catch and pause briefly with your oars feathered before squaring and planting them. A less-challenging version of this drill can be done while rowing the release: at the end of your shortened recovery, you pause before squaring your oars. Because your oar shafts will be perpendicular to the boat and because it won't have been long since you released them from the water, your boat should still be quite stable, making your pause at the catch less scary than it otherwise would be. Doing this drill, then, can be a good first step toward acquiring the ability to row "with authority"—to row, that is, so that it is you, not your boat, that dictates when you plant your blades.

THE PROBLEM(S) WITH SPLASHING

It is tempting to dismiss splashing as a purely cosmetic defect in rowing form. We should not give in to this temptation, though. Splashing negatively impacts a boat in many different ways. Allow me to describe some of them.

Usually, when a rower splashes at the catch, the splash moves toward the bow of the boat. Because of the law of conservation of momentum, though, anything that moves toward the bow of the boat impedes the forward progress of that boat. Thus, bow-ward splashing slows a boat down.

But this is only one of many problems that splashing causes. If you row in a double or quad and splash, that splash (unless you are rowing bow) will likely spray the rower unfortunate enough to sit behind you. He might end up drenched. This will make him unhappy, especially if the day is cold or you are rowing in a polluted lake or river.

Besides affecting the morale of your boat mates, your splashing can affect boat performance. The person who sits behind you will probably end up with hands that, because they are wet from your splashing, are far more likely to slip while squaring and feathering the oars. This slipping can result in crabs being caught, which will slow down the boat. And if the weather is cold when you soak your boat mate, his hands are likely to go numb, in which case he might lose possession of an oar handle. This can *really* slow down the boat.

Often, a splasher will be blissfully unaware of her splashing; it affects, after all, someone else. This clueless splasher might even feel superior to the person who sits behind her in the boat: he is such a klutz, always catching crabs and losing his oars. But in fact, it is the splasher who is ultimately responsible for this innocent bystander's klutziness.

It would be bad enough if the harm done to the splashed individual ended when the row did. Suppose, though, that as a result of rowing with wet hands, this individual gets new blisters. He will find himself, on subsequent days, rowing with raw flesh, and as a result might hold his oar handles differently, in an attempt to protect the affected areas. Because of this altered grip, he might catch crabs that, had he not been splashed, he would easily have avoided. Think of it: even though he has abandoned the splasher as a rowing partner, the splashing he endured is still slowing him down. Oh, the humanity!

This brings us to the last entry on my list of the problems caused by splashing. Splashed water, whether it ends up in the clothing of your boat mates or sloshing around in the hull of the boat, will add to the weight of the boat. This will cause the boat to ride lower in the water, increasing hull drag, which in turn will slow the boat down. And not only that, but if the boat is a quad, the water you splashed into it will come pouring out when you and your boat mates lift it out of the water: you will all get an involuntary shower that, on a cold autumn morning, can be quite bracing. Even the people you didn't splash will end up getting wet.

Splashing, it should by now be clear, is a wonderful way to make yourself unpopular in a boat. And splashing is easy to avoid: you need only hold your hand an inch or two lower going into the catch. Why, then, would anyone splash? In most cases, flipophobia is the most plausible explanation: people splash because they find it psychologically impossible to raise their blades at the catch.

POSTURE AT THE CATCH

So far, we have talked about what your blades are doing at the catch. Now let us turn our attention to what your torso is doing.

The catch takes place at the end of the recovery. At that point, your body will be toward the stern end of the slide, but just how far toward it should you be? The consensus view is that you should slide sternward until your shins are vertical. If they go past vertical, you will be guilty of "over-compressing." This is undesirable because once your shins are past vertical, the pushing ability of your legs starts to decline. Also, if you over-compress, you increase your chances of coming off the seat.

It is, to be sure, difficult for a rower to know, while he is rowing, how much his shins are sloping. If the tracks of his boat are adjustable, though, a rower can set them so his seat "stops out"* an inch or so past when his shins are vertical. Then, if he

---

*At the ends of the slide, there are "stops" that prevent your seat from coming off the track. If your seat wheels make contact with one of these, you are said to have "stopped out."

feels his seat hit the stern stop, he will know he is over-compressing.

At the catch, a rower should be leaning forward at the waist so his torso makes an oblique angle with the stern deck. Although there is such a thing as too much *body angle*, as it is called, many rowers have too little. In some cases, it is because they are inflexible and therefore have trouble bending at the waist. Such rowers should do exercises to increase their flexibility; yoga is wonderful for this. In other cases, rowers have trouble bending from the waist because of a weight problem. The obvious solution is to lose the weight, perhaps by eating less and better—and rowing more.

Rowers, I should add, pay twice, in terms of boat performance, for being overweight. Their inability to reach at the catch will shorten their drive and thereby diminish the power they can apply to the oars, and their extra pounds will cause the boat to ride lower in the water than it needs to, thereby increasing hull drag and slowing down the boat.

One other thought about weight: there are no overweight Formula One racecar drivers. This is because they know that added ounces have an impact on car performance. If they, with their 800-horsepower engines worry about ounces, shouldn't rowers, with their one person-power engines, worry about pounds?

At the catch, a rower will be at the stern-end of his slide, leaning forward from the waist, with his arms completely outstretched. As a result, his hands will be outside the hull of the boat. His goal should be to have a large catch angle—at least 60 degrees. (This would result in his oar shafts, at the catch, being only 30 degrees from the hull of the boat.) As I have explained, though, many rowers, because of their fear of flipping, find this hard to do.

OVERCOMING ANATOMICAL DISCRIMINATION

A large catch angle comes easier for some rowers than for others. In particular, someone with a rower's body—someone, that is, with long legs, a long torso, long arms, and broad shoulders*—will find it anatomically easy to get his hands way out of

---

*It might not be obvious what effect shoulder breadth will have on catch angle, but for a given arm length, the broader your shoulders are, the longer your "wingspan" will be, and therefore the farther you will be able to reach at the catch.

the boat at the catch and thereby achieve a large catch angle. Suppose, though, that instead of having a rower's body, you have a jockey's body, with short legs, a short torso, narrow shoulders, and short arms. In order for you to have an adequate catch angle, you must concentrate on two things.

First, you must develop the ability to lean way forward at the catch. Along these lines, it is instructive to compare the rowing styles of elite male and female rowers. Watch rowing videos, and you will see that women rowers tend, at the catch, to lean farther forward than men do; indeed, they lean so far that their shoulders come almost into contact with their knees. They do this in part because, thanks to their greater flexibility, women *can* lean farther. One also suspects, though, that given their generally shorter stature, it is what they *must* do to have an adequate catch angle.

Even with their aggressive leaning, though, women rowers don't quite make up the stature gap: they have about four degrees less catch angle, on average, than men. (And lightweight women, who tend to be the shortest women, have about six degrees less catch angle than openweight men, who tend to be the tallest men.)

The second thing rowers who are relatively small need to concentrate on is becoming confident at the catch. In most cases, if a rower has a small catch angle, it isn't her body that is constraining her; it is her mind. More precisely, flipophobia is causing her to catch prematurely. Thus, it becomes imperative for short rowers to overcome their flipophobia. I should add that the shorter a rower is, the less "top-heavy" and therefore the more stable her boat will be. It is therefore easier for light, short people to set a boat, meaning that it will be easier for them to become confident at the catch.

Rowing is by its very nature a sport that discriminates anatomically: it favors tall people over short people. Nevertheless, it is possible for a short person, by developing waist flexibility and confidence at the catch, to achieve a bigger catch angle than many tall rowers have. Do this, and a person with the jockey's body might subsequently be able, in races, to experience the satisfaction of leaving those with rower's bodies in her wake.

TURNING THE BOAT

As we have seen, a rower's hands should be horizontally symmetrical, with the left hand directly across from the right throughout the stroke. The exception to the horizontal-symmetry rule is if you want to turn your boat. This leaves us with an interesting question: what is the best way to break symmetry in order to turn? Suppose, for the sake of concreteness, that you want to turn your boat to the right.

I would argue, to begin with, that the best *time* to break symmetry is at the catch. This is when your blades will be as close to the bow as they ever will, meaning that as you start your drive, most of their motion will be away from the bow. Thus, reaching farther with one blade at the catch will have the effect of pushing laterally on the bow of the boat and will therefore be the most effective way to change the boat's heading.

Besides this "scientific" reason for choosing the catch as the best time to break symmetry, there are technical reasons as well. To explore these reasons, let us consider some of the other ways you might turn a boat.

You might, to begin with, try to turn your boat to the right not by reaching farther at the catch with your left hand but by pulling harder on your left oar *during the drive*. This will indeed cause your boat to veer to the right, but it will also cause your left oar handle to arrive at your abdomen before your right handle does. Now what? Your left blade needs to come out of the water immediately, or its presence there will check the forward motion of the boat and will probably even make the boat swerve, perversely, to the left.

You could remove your left blade first and then, a split second later, remove your right, but I suspect that most rowers would find this sequential release technique—first one blade, then the other—difficult to master.

How about turning the boat not by breaking horizontal symmetry at the catch and not by pulling asymmetrically during the drive, but by breaking horizontal symmetry *at the release*? Do this, and your hands would be symmetrical until the last few inches of your drive. At that point, you would release your right blade while continuing to drive with your left. In other words, you would release your right blade when your right handle was still a few inches away from your abdomen and release your left blade a split second later, when your left handle was nearly at your abdomen. This would shorten the drive of your right blade, while leaving the drive of your left blade its usual length, which in turn would cause your boat to veer to the right.

As I have said, though, rowers will find it difficult to sequentially release their blades, and even if they can learn to do so, this technique has the disadvantage of failing to utilize several inches of right-blade drive, something a speed-obsessed rower will be reluctant to do.

These aren't, however, the only ways to turn a boat. Novice rowers, for example, routinely turn their boat by rowing with one oar while feathering the other, or by rowing with one oar while checking the other. These are techniques, once again, that racers would be reluctant to use.

Thus, reaching farther with one hand at the catch is arguably the best way to turn a boat. As it so happens, though, there is more than one way to reach farther with one hand at the catch, meaning that our discussion of how to turn a boat is not yet complete.

You can, to begin with, reach farther with your left hand than your right simply by reaching less far with your right hand than you normally do. The obvious way to accomplish this is by crooking your right elbow a bit going into the catch. Doing this, however, will shorten the drive of your right blade, thereby decreasing the power it provides. A second way to reach farther with your left hand is to rotate your torso clockwise (as seen from above) going into the catch. Again, though, doing this will shorten the drive of your right blade: by rotating your torso, you move your right hand back as much as you move your left hand forward. Not only that, but rotating your torso in this manner can disturb the set of the boat—just when, as we have seen, that set is most precarious. A third way to reach farther with your left hand is by leaning your whole torso to the left as you come into the catch, but in terms of boat set, this is an even worse idea than rotating your torso.

I routinely encounter rowers who tell me that they turn their boat by pushing harder with one foot than the other during the drive. It is hard to see, though, how such an action could turn a boat unless the asymmetrical pushing was causing an asymmetry in their body posture, meaning that it was *really* the posture asymmetry that was turning their boat. Indeed, I have experimented with this. I have rowed with one foot out of its shoe so that I was pushing with only one foot. Nevertheless, as long as I consciously kept my upper body symmetrical, the boat moved straight as an arrow, albeit with less power.

What we rowers need, then, is a way to reach farther with our left hand than with our right, but without significantly shortening the distance our right hand reaches and without jeopardizing the set of our boat. The key to accomplishing this, I think, is the effective use of our shoulders.

Our shoulders are more flexible than we give them credit for being. To explore their flexibility, stand with your back against a doorjamb, with both arms held horizontally in front of you. Now, while keeping your spine against the jamb, move your shoulders as far forward as you can and then as far back as you can. I don't regard myself as being particularly flexible, and yet when I do this experiment, my fingertips shift position by nearly a foot.

Rowers might not realize it, but if they are reaching fully at the catch, their shoulders will be pushed forward in the manner I have described. And to be absolutely clear about this, the rowers' shoulders won't be *shrugged upward*; that would be a waste of energy. They will instead be *curled forward*.

To turn the boat without bending an elbow and without rotating the torso, a rower need only curl farther forward with one shoulder than the other. Yes, he will be losing a bit of drive on the shoulder that doesn't get curled forward, but that is the price of turning the boat: there must be a break in symmetry that results in one oar delivering more power than the other.

Someone might complain that the "reaching farther" technique for turning boats won't allow a rower to make dramatic changes in direction. I agree entirely but will quickly add that under normal racing circumstances,* there shouldn't be any need to make dramatic turns. Usually, a need to make such turns is evidence that a rower has allowed his boat to veer off course—probably because he has been rowing in an asymmetric manner.

THE CATCH DISSECTED

Let us now turn our attention back to straight-line rowing. Suppose you are at the catch. Your oar blades have been squared without kicking up any splash. Now you "catch water" by dropping your blades into it. This sounds easy, but things quickly get complicated.

---

*One exception is head racing on courses that require the equivalent of right-angle turns. (I have raced on such courses.) Another exception is "stake racing," in which a racer rows up a course, rounds a buoy, and then rows back. I have never stake-raced, but I have on occasion attempted to round a buoy at speed. All I can say is that doing this well is an art unto itself.

There are coaches who instruct athletes to literally *drop* their oars into the water—to let gravity pull them down. Research by Kleshnev indicates, however, that although rowers might get away with this while paddling at a super-slow stroke rate, it won't work very well in regular rowing. This is because it would take gravity about 0.3 of a second to get the blades completely planted, and by that time, in normal rowing, one-third of the drive would be over and would have been underutilized by the not-yet-fully-submerged blade.*

To have an effective catch, then, a rower must *plunge* his blades into the water by lifting up on the oar handles. About four inches (ten cm) of lift should be adequate. And at the same time as he is raising them, he will want to be pulling those handles toward him. Allow me to explain why.

Suppose that a rower, after squaring his blades at the catch, lowers them by lifting his hands straight up. His blades will then be moving neither toward the bow nor the stern of the boat. The problem is that as long as the boat is moving, the water will be moving toward the stern of the boat, meaning that when the lower edge of the blade comes into contact with the water, a splash will result. To avoid this phenomenon, the rower must make the blade speed match the water speed, and the way to do this is to *pull back on the handle of the oar at the same time as he is lifting up on that handle.* He should pull back enough so that from the blade's point of view, the water into which it is sinking is stationary. Thus, the handles of the oars, instead of going straight up, will simultaneously move up and toward the rower, along a little incline. This will cause the blades to go down and toward the stern of the boat, along a corresponding incline.

How fast the rower should pull back on the handles during the catch will obviously depend on how fast the boat is moving: the faster the boat, the faster the blades will have to move, meaning the faster the handles will have to move. If the handles are moving too slowly toward the rower, there will be a splash toward the bow, and if the handles are moving too quickly toward the rower, there will be a splash toward the stern.† If the

---

Rowing Biomechanics Newsletter (April, 2007).

†A splash toward the bow of the boat is clearly a bad thing, since water thrown forward saps the momentum of the boat. A splash toward the stern does not raise the same issue. Indeed, coaches who want rowers to be very aggressive during the early part of the drive—to "hit the catch hard"—have no problem with a slight splash toward the stern.

blade is moving at just the right speed, though, there will be very little splash* and almost no noise.

This way of splashing at the catch, it should be noted, is different from the other ways we have considered. In those ways, the feathered blade was too close to the water when the rower squared it. As a result, the bottom edge of the blade touched the water and a splash resulted. When you fail to match blade speed to water speed, though, it isn't the *squaring of the blade* that kicks up a splash; it is the *squared blade itself*, being lowered into the water.

Thus, although rowers might talk about *the* problem of splashing at the catch, there are in fact *three different ways* to splash. You can drag your oars throughout the recovery, causing you to splash when you square them; you can have a touch-and-go catch, which again will cause you to splash when you square your blades; or you can square your blades without splashing, but then kick up a splash by lowering those blades into what is, from their point of view, moving water.

To match blade speed to water speed will cost a rower: he will have to be moving his blades sternward before applying full power to them. A speed-conscious rower will want to minimize this sternward motion, and as a result, he will want to plant his blades quickly. According to Kleshnev, a very good rower might use up only 4 degrees of sweep angle to get his blades fully submerged; he will, in rowing terminology, have only 4 degrees of *catch slip*.† He can accomplish this by pulling his handles toward him by 2-3 inches (5-8 cm) while lowering them.

OTHER CATCH DEFECTS

Suppose a rower succeeds in matching the speed of the blades at the catch to the water speed. There won't be any post-squaring splash, but mistakes are still possible.

In what I shall call a *shallow catch*, a blade isn't fully submerged before the rower starts pulling on the oar handle in earnest. This will cause an air gap to open up behind the semi-submerged blade. What happens next depends on whether the

---

*Notice that if a rower has a good catch angle, the blades of his oars will, at the catch, be "pointed into" the oncoming water, which will reduce splash.

†*Rowing Biomechanics Newsletter* (April, 2007).

blade remains too shallow or submerges to proper depth. If it remains too shallow, the blade will pull through the water and a tearing noise will result. If the blade continues its descent, the air gap will fill with water and a distinctive *kerplunk* noise will result.

The solution to shallow catches is obvious: wait until the blades are submerged before you apply power to the oar handles. If the blades are symmetrically too shallow, just raise the oar handles a bit more at the catch before you turn on the power. I think it is more common, though, for the blades to be asymmetrically too shallow. More precisely, I think that what often happens is that a rower will apply power when his right blade is properly submerged but his left blade isn't. The result will be a *kerplunk* noise on the left but no noise on the right. It is also likely that a boat in which the left blade is routinely kerplunking will have a tendency to veer in that direction. This is because the first inches of the left-blade drive will be less effective than the first inches of the right-blade drive. A longer drive on the right than the left will cause the boat to veer to the left.

The reason left-blades tend to kerplunk is that rowers make the mistake of bringing their left hand to the same level as their right at the catch. As we have seen, a rower's left hand should be higher than his right throughout the stroke. Do this, and as long as the boat is level, his blades will be the same distance above the water during the recovery. By moving his left hand to the same height as his right in preparation for the catch, though, a rower will unwittingly raise his left blade higher than his right. Then, if he raises both hands the same distance at the catch, and if he raises his right hand far enough to properly submerge the right blade, the left blade won't yet be fully submerged. If he applies power at this moment, the right blade will be ready, but the left blade won't, and a kerplunk will result.

In what I have called a *shallow* catch, a rower applies power to his blades before they are completely submerged. In what I shall call a *slow catch*, by way of contrast, he waits until his blades are submerged to apply power, but submerges them very, very slowly. We have seen that an elite rower might have only 4 degrees of catch slip. An average rower might have 10 degrees. A rower with a slow catch, though, might have 20 or even 30 degrees of catch slip.

During this lengthy blade-lowering process, the rower's blades will be moving at the same speed as the water, and as a result, there will be no splash. And there won't be the kerplunk or tearing noise that you expect to hear when power is applied to half-submerged blades.* This is because power isn't yet being applied! The blades, slowly descending into the water, will resemble a person easing himself into a too-hot bathtub.

The cure to a slow catch is simple: at the catch, raise the hands quickly to completely submerge the blades and then, without any delay, apply power to them. If a rower is accustomed to a slow catch, he will find that doing this dramatically increases the power he expends on each stroke and thereby makes rowing much more difficult—which might be one of the reasons he developed a slow catch in the first place.

Some rowers plant their oars quickly but start raising them out of the water well before the release. They do this by lowering their hands in the last third of the drive. But again, if their half-extracted blades don't start tearing through the water, it is evidence that they aren't applying much power to their oars.

Blades should remain submerged until the very end of the drive, at which point they should come out quickly and start moving bow-ward. One reason rowers start raising their blades prematurely during the drive is because doing so simplifies their release. It also deprives them, though, of the power they could have obtained from the final portion of the drive.

---

*Although most technical mistakes in rowing have a distinctive noise that is associated with them, a slow catch is an exception: it is utterly silent. So is the mistake of rowing with blades too deep.

EIGHT

The Drive

Suppose you have properly caught water: at the end of the recovery, you have squared your blades and then quickly and completely submerged them, all without wasting any time or making much of a splash. You will, at this point, be at the stern end of the slide, bending forward at the waist, with your hands reaching out of the boat. It is time to apply full power to your oar handles and thereby begin your drive.

The first half of the drive is critical to the performance of a boat. It is when the blades of the oars can take advantage of hydrodynamic lift—more on this later. It is also when the leg muscles, which provide most of the power delivered in a stroke, are active. A rower cannot afford to waste this power, and yet that is precisely what many rowers do.

Some of these rowers make the mistake of "shooting their slide": they start pushing back with their legs, causing their seat to move toward the bow of the boat, without simultaneously pulling on the handles of the oars. They accomplish this trick by leaning farther forward from their waist as their seat slides back. By the time they get around to pulling on the oar handles, their butt will be sticking out. For this reason, "shooting the slide" is also called "shooting your tail."

The slide-shooting rower is using his powerful quadriceps to lean forward from the waist, something he could easily do without involving his quadriceps—indeed, something he should have done way back at the release, when his legs were still fully extended. Having shot his slide, the rower has only his back and arms left to pull the oars. Even taken together, though, his back and arms aren't as powerful as his legs. What a waste!

In cycling, legs play an even more important role than they do in rowing. To make the most of the power provided by their legs, cyclists favor a bicycle frame that is rigid: if it flexed when they pedaled, energy that could go into moving the bike forward would instead be diverted into flexing the frame. Cyclists also use rigid metal crank arms to transmit the power their legs supply into a sprocket, which in turn transmits that power to the rear wheel by means of an unstretchable chain. Imagine how hard it would be to propel a bicycle that had rubber crank arms and a rubber belt in place of a chain! Much of the cyclist's energy would be wasted flexing the crank arms and stretching the belt. It would feel like riding a bicycle through sand.

Rowers, by way of contrast, don't have the luxury of being able to transmit power by means of a rigid crank arm and unstretchable chain. Instead, the power of a rower's legs is transmitted through flesh and bone. It travels through his hips, up his back, down his arms, along his oars, and finally into the water. (And as it so happens, not even his oar shafts are rigid, the way a bicycle crank arm is; instead, they are designed to flex a bit during the drive.) This means that vast amounts of leg power can be dissipated in a rower's body before it reaches the water. Indeed, it can waste almost all of the power his legs generate. This is what happens when a rower severely shoots his slide.

In a severe case of slide-shooting, a rower's seat might move back two feet before his oar handles start moving. This sort of thing is unheard of in advanced rowers, but they might make a subtler version of the same mistake. If they fail to "lock" their back—or more accurately, *engage* it—before they start pushing with their legs, their seat will move a few inches bow-ward before their oar handles start moving. Let us refer to this as a *soft shoot*. A rower with this problem won't be wasting power as extravagantly as a rower with a full-blown case of slide-shooting, but he will still be wasting power. The solution to a soft shoot is simple: don't let the wheels of your slide turn until your back is engaged. And better still, don't let the wheels of your slide turn until your back is engaged *and your blades are submerged*; otherwise you will encounter the catch problems described in the previous chapter.

The ratio between oar-handle-motion and seat-motion is, by the way, a wonderful indicator of how efficiently, early in the drive,* a rower's body is transmitting the power his legs are gen-

---

*This metric is not useful later in the drive. As the drive progresses, after all, the rower's legs play a diminished role. Indeed, after his legs are fully extended, and his seat thereupon comes to a halt, the drive continues, with his back and arms left to complete the job his legs began. Thus, the ratio between oar-handle motion and seat motion will increase as the drive progresses, and will become infinite when his seat stops moving.

erating. If a rower shoots his slide, this ratio will be less than one: his oar handles won't move as far bow-ward as his seat will. If you think about the (idealized) geometry of the situation, the only way this can happen is if the rower's torso leans further forward as his legs push, which represents a waste of energy. If, however, a rower keeps his body rigid during the drive, the ratio between oar-handle-motion and seat-motion will equal one, meaning that for every centimeter of bow-ward seat movement, the oar handles will move bow-ward by one centimeter.

A "Flexed" Back

Rowers often think their backs are ramrod straight going into the catch, but if you examine side-angle videos of them, you will find that they almost always curl their back, the way a scared cat would. It is very difficult for rowers with normal flexibility to avoid doing this. But one thing rowers can do is attempt to "flex" their lower back at the end of the recovery. In other words, a rower should tilt his pelvis slightly forward in an attempt to make his back do the opposite of what a scared cat's back does. And I say "attempt" because it is very unlikely that he will succeed. It will still look, from the side, like he is hunching his back, but a bit less than was formerly the case.

And why go to the trouble of flexing his lower back going into the catch? Because a flexed lower back will be "engaged," meaning that the power provided by his legs will get transmitted into his oars instead of being squandered making his torso lean forward.

One way a rower can ensure the flexing of his back is to keep his chin up going into the catch; it is, after all, hard to keep your chin up unless you are simultaneously flexing your back. And because his back is flexed, the rower's chest will thrust forward. With chin held high and chest puffed out, he will look like he is proud of his rowing, as well he should be. Or, if you don't like this simile, here is another: he will look, going into the catch, as if he were doing a swan dive.

It is important, as we have seen, for rowers to reach out of the boat at the catch in order to have a big catch angle. Flexing his back in the manner I have described, though, makes it harder for a rower to do this. Indeed, by curling his back like that of a scared cat, he can get a few more inches of reach. So why not curl? Because by doing so, he gives up more than he gains. Yes, curling his back might let him reach a bit farther, but it also increases the chance that, because his back isn't engaged, he will have a "soft shoot" when he begins his drive, and the power wasted by the soft shoot will arguably exceed the power gained by the extended reach.

The Drive Commences

A rower, let us imagine, is at the end of the recovery. He is leaning forward from his waist, with his lower back flexed in the manner described above and with his arms outstretched. His blades have been squared and are ready to be planted in the water. Now what?

In our discussion of the catch, we saw that a rower, besides raising his handles to lower his blades into the water, should pull back slightly on those handles so the blades will be stationary relative to the water they are entering; otherwise, they will kick up a splash when they encounter the water. This raises the question of how best to do this initial pulling. The available sources of pulling power are the arms, legs, and back. Which of these should a rower employ?

He should *not* use his arms; he should not, that is, "break" his elbows to pull his handles closer to his body. Do this, and he will put his arms in a tug of war against his legs and back, and it is a war that his arms will surely lose. Instead, he should "open up" his body angle a bit. He should, in other words, slightly increase the angle between his torso and the stern deck of the boat. Doing this, besides causing his blades to become stationary relative to the water they are entering, will help prevent the rower from shooting his slide at the catch.*

As soon as his blades are fully submerged, the rower should start pushing with his legs. If he has properly prepared for this moment, his body will act like a rigid crank arm on a bicycle: the power provided by his legs will be efficiently transmitted through his body, into his oar handles, and thereby to the blades.

---

*Earlier I said that for each centimeter the seat moves bow-ward early in the drive, the oar handles should move one centimeter bow-ward. If, however, we take into account the fact that the rower is opening up his body angle early in the drive, we might find that his oar handles move *more* than one centimeter bow-ward.

ROWING ASYMMETRICALLY DEEP

I have already described the sorts of problems caused by the blades being asymmetrical during the drive. If the blades aren't horizontally symmetrical, the boat will either constantly veer in one direction or will "wag its tail," neither of which is desirable. If the blades aren't vertically symmetrical, one blade will end up deeper than the other. This might mean that one blade is submerged to the proper depth and the other is partly out of the water. The submerged blade will provide more power than the partially submerged blade, causing the boat to veer. Or it might mean that although both blades are submerged, one is submerged more deeply than the other. In this case, the boat will not only veer but will probably rock as well. Allow me to explain why.

It would be possible to move a boat through the water using oars whose blades have been sawed off. This is because the shafts themselves have drag—not as much drag as a blade* but enough to move a boat. Someone might argue that, given that this is the case, a rower might as well take advantage of the shafts' drag by submerging them during the drive. The problem with this idea is that unlike blades, shafts are symmetrical.

Oar *blades* have lots of drag when moved face-on through the water but very little drag when moved edge-on into it. This means that squared blades go into and out of the water easily, but go through the water with difficulty—just the combination of characteristics a rower needs. Oar *shafts*, on the other hand, exhibit the same drag when they go into and out of the water as they do going horizontally through the water. Not only that, but whereas blades are pretty close to neutral buoyancy, shafts are quite buoyant—indeed, buoyant enough that the Coast Guard has approved them as flotation devices. Thus, submerge one or both shafts during the drive, and there will be consequences.

Suppose, to begin with, that at the catch, a rower plants his right blade so the top is just below the surface, meaning that very little of the shaft is submerged, but plants his left blade deep

---

*People normally don't think of a blade as having drag. More generally, people think of drag as a bad thing, if speed is your goal. And yet, unless an oar blade had considerable drag—unless, that is, it resisted moving face-on through the water—its usefulness in propelling a boat would be limited.

enough that half the shaft is submerged. Doing this will affect the set of the boat: the left shaft being pushed into and then extracted from the water will cause the boat to rock. If you don't believe me, try this experiment: in a stationary boat, with blades squared and at hands-away, see what happens when you start plunging one blade half-shaft deep into and out of the water, while keeping the other blade near the surface. The boat will rock in a most impressive manner.

In my activities as coach, I periodically go out in a double with someone who rows asymmetrically deep. As long as we row slowly, the boat will be nicely set, but once we start applying power, it will start to rock. As a result, blades will start splashing and dragging, and whatever confidence we might have had at the catch will be shattered. Asymmetrically deep blades, I tell rowers, are like an off-balance washing machine. When the drum first starts spinning to remove water, things will be okay, but as the rate of spinning increases, the effect of even a small asymmetry in the distribution of the laundry can cause the machine first to vibrate and then to lurch wildly.

Rowing with one blade deeper than the other, besides causing a boat to rock, will cause it to veer. I first became aware of this phenomenon during a coached-double outing. I was rowing bow, and the athlete I was coaching was rowing stroke. The boat kept veering to the right; indeed, it was all I could do to pull longer with my right oar to keep the boat on course. At first, I suspected that the boat had a bent skeg. Then I realized that during the drive, the other rower was rowing with his right blade at the proper depth but with his left blade more than half-shaft deep. The propulsive force of this shaft was considerable.

It is almost always the case, by the way, that if a rower rows with one blade asymmetrically deeper than the other, the left blade will be the deep one, as was the case with the rower just described. Notice, after all, that if the rower's hands are horizontally symmetrical, his right hand must spend crossover "confined" between his left hand and his lap. Not only that, but when it is outside of crossover, his right hand will either have just emerged from confinement or be just about to enter it. It is therefore difficult for his right hand to drift too high during the drive. His left hand, by way of contrast, is limited by his right hand in how low it can go, but there is no limit to how high it can go. This in turn means that his left blade will, unless the rower is vigilant, have a tendency to go too deep during the drive.

This isn't, by the way, the only problem that the relative freedom of their left hand causes rowers. I have found that if rowers drag only one oar during the recovery, it is likely to be their left oar. Likewise, if rowers splash with only one oar at the catch, it is likely to be their left oar.

Having said this, I should add that it *is* possible for a rower's left blade to be too shallow during the drive. In particular, this will happen if a rower mistakenly thinks that to keep his blades at the same height above or below the water, he has to keep his hands at the same height. Such a rower will deal with crossover by breaking horizontal symmetry: he might, for example, keep his right hand closer to his body than his left throughout the stroke: his right hand will lead his left during the drive and follow it during the recovery. But since boats are rigged so that a rower has to keep his left hand higher than his right in order to keep his blades level, this rower's left blade, instead of being too deep during the drive, will end up too shallow.

I have said it before, but it merits repeating: *to keep his blades symmetrical, a rower should keep his hands horizontally symmetrical but with his left hand always a few inches higher than his right, from the catch, to the release, and back to the catch again.*

ROWING SYMMETRICALLY TOO DEEP

It is clearly a mistake to row with blades that are asymmetrically deep—with, for example, one blade just under the surface but the other submerged half-shaft deep. But as long as the blades are *symmetrically* deep, why not plant them as deep as you can? I have above described the propulsive power of a submerged shaft. Why not take advantage of this power by rowing with *both* blades submerged half-shaft deep? Doing this wouldn't cause the rocking or veering problems I have described, so why not do it?

Although symmetrically deep rowing will indeed avoid certain problems, it can give rise to others. If blades go deep during the drive, it is harder to extract them at the release, and unless you have excellent timing, you will likely catch crabs as a result. This problem is common among Learn to Row students. To encourage them to row shallow, I tell them that crabs are deep-dwelling creatures; indeed, they are reluctant to come within ten inches of the surface. Thus, if students keep their blades in the top ten inches of the water, they can become almost crab proof.

A skilled rower will have mastered the timing of the release and therefore won't have a crab problem. He will, however, encounter another problem: rowing with blades that are symmetrically too deep is likely to cause the boat to bob up and down. We have seen that rowing with one blade deeper than the other can cause the boat to rock: the too-deep blade will, after all, tend to raise that side of the boat when it is being pushed into the water and lower that side of the boat when it is being pulled out of the water. Row with *both* blades too deep, though, and *both* sides of the boat will be raised at the beginning of the drive and lowered at the end, and the result will be a bobbing boat.

And why is bobbing bad? Because energy spent making a boat bob up and down is wasted energy. Rowers can get an idea of how much energy bobbing wastes by doing what might be called a *reverse-tap drill.* In a stationary boat, move your oars to hands away, square them, and then let them float. In a regular tap-at-hands-away drill, you would now lift your blades out of the water and then let them descend to flotation depth again. Doing this requires very little effort; indeed, the blades can be raised and lowered with a single finger. In a reverse-tap drill, though, you plunge the blades down until, say, half of the shaft is submerged, pull the blades back up to flotation depth, and then plunge them under again. You will be able to feel your boat moving up and down as you do this, and you might see waves radiating out from your hull as a result.

To appreciate how much energy deep blades waste, do the above drill not just for 10 reverse taps or even 100, but for 600, which is the number of strokes you might take in a 5000-meter head race. Your expenditure of energy will be significant, and in spending this up-and-down energy, you will not have moved your boat forward by a single inch.

It would be one thing if a rower simply wasted energy by bobbing a boat. A case can be made, though, that the bobbing motion increases hull drag: when the boat "bobs down," after all, more of the hull will be in contact with the water. In other words, a case can be made that by making the boat bob, you are expending energy to make the boat harder to propel. Not a good racing strategy!

Advocates of "deep rowing" might, at this point, argue that although it is true that a bobbing boat will ride deeper than normal during some parts of the stroke, it will ride higher than normal at others, and this higher riding will more than offset the deeper riding, in terms of hull drag. The boat, as a result, will be faster than it otherwise would. I am not an expert in hydrodynamics, but I strongly suspect that because hull drag affects boat speed in an exponential manner, this claim is false.*

At this point, an advocate of deep rowing might tell us that even if making the boat bob does increase hull drag a bit, the extra power you can apply by involving the shafts in the drive more than makes up for this drag. The rower in question might tell us that in order to take full advantage of the power at his disposal, he has to make use not only of his blades but his shafts as well.

In response to this suggestion, I would tell the rower that there is a much more elegant solution to his problem: get oars with bigger blades! Blades are designed to move easily into and out of the water; shafts aren't. And if he can't get a bigger blade, he can always increase the load on his current oars by moving the button closer to the handle. Either of these solutions would avoid making his boat bob and would therefore be a better solution than rowing with his shafts submerged.

ROWING WITH "LEVEL HANDS"

We have already discussed the issue of proper hand separation at crossover: your hands should be held so that there is an inch or so of air space between them during the crossover portion of the drive. (I accomplish this by keeping the top of my left hand about four inches above the top of my right.) We have also seen that in a properly rigged boat, your blades will be symmetrical as long as you keep your hands horizontally symmetrical and maintain the proper height difference between them.

As it so happens, though, proper hand separation can be maintained over a wide range of hand heights. Your right hand can be down on your lap, at armpit height, or anywhere in be-

---

*Coaches and rowers sometimes talk about the things they can do, both at the start of a race and on each stroke thereafter, to get a boat "up and out of the water." This issue also arises when they are deciding how to set the trim of the boat: is it better for weight to be distributed so that the bow rides higher than the stern, or should the bow ride lower than the stern? They know that boats that hydroplane are much faster than boats that don't, and they try to figure out how to get the boats they row to do a low-grade form of hydroplaning. The question, of course, is whether energy spent "lifting" the boat is compensated for, in terms of boat speed, by the reduction in the drag of the "lifted" boat. It is a subject of considerable debate.

tween. In each case, as long as you keep the top of your left hand about four inches above the top of your right, the blades of your oars will be vertically symmetrical. The question, then, is how high your hands should be during the drive, which is equivalent to asking how deep your blades should be.

I have already described the problem that arises if the blades are symmetrically half-shaft deep: the boat will bob. It is also clear that rowers shouldn't row with their blades halfway out of the water: such blades would not provide much propulsion. But where, between being half-shaft deep and halfway out of the water, is the best place for blades to be during the drive?

I would argue that a rower's goal, during the drive, should be to keep her blades at their flotation depth.* As we saw in chapter 5, she can ascertain this depth by sitting in a stationary boat on flat water, moving her hands to "hands away," squaring her blades, and then *almost* releasing her grip on the handles so that her blades are essentially floating in the water. (When the oars I use are at flotation depth, their top edge is about an inch above the waterline.) Her goal should be to keep her blades this deep throughout the drive.

To accomplish this goal, it helps for her to know her catch and release targets. To find the former, she should go forward to the catch and let her squared blades find their flotation depth. She should note the positions of her hands. These are her *catch targets*—where her hands should be when she begins her drive. If her boat is level and properly rigged, the catch target of her left hand will be a few inches higher than the catch target of her right. (For a wonderful illustration of this difference in hand height, look at the rower on the cover of this book.)

Now she should slowly pull her squared blades back to the release and again let them float. She should again note the position of her hands against her abdomen. These are her *release targets*—where her hands should be when she ends her drive. Again, the release target of her left hand will be a few inches higher on her abdomen than the release target of her right.

---

*If she does this in a boat that is level and rigged properly, her hands will have the proper vertical separation; there will, in other words, be an inch or so of air space between them. If there isn't, she needs to adjust her rigging. In particular, if there is too little air space, she needs to raise her left oarlock relative to her right. (Do this, and she will have to lift her left hand higher to bring her left blade back down to flotation depth.)

To keep her blades at flotation depth throughout the drive, she need only plant them to flotation depth at the catch and then pull *straight back* on her oars until her hands reach their release targets. Her hands, in other words, should move along a path that is parallel to the surface of the water. Do this, and she will be rowing with what coaches call *level hands*.*

Many rowers fail to row with level hands. Because they have poor blade control, novice rowers tend initially to row too shallow. Then they tend to overcorrect for this mistake and start rowing too deep. More precisely, they row so that their blade spends the first half of the drive diving deeper and the second half trying to get back to the surface.

Their blades do this because they raise their hands in the first half of the drive and then lower them in the second half. It looks like they are rowing over an imaginary barrel that someone has inconveniently left in their lap. They do this, I think, because their timing is off. A rower with proper form will first push with her legs, then start pulling with her back, and finally start pulling with her arms. But if a rower involves her back and arms too soon, her knees will still be sticking up into the air and she will have to raise her hands to get over them. She is thus figuratively "rowing over a barrel" by literally rowing over her knees.

Intermediate-level rowers also have a tendency to row over the barrel. They do this not because they have the timing problem that novice rowers do. Instead, they do it, I think, because they are convinced that by involving their shafts in the drive, they can provide more forward propulsion to the boat than if they use their blades alone. They are right in thinking this, but as we have seen, there are problems with using shafts as blades. In other cases, intermediate-level rowers do not intend to row deep in the middle of the drive. They do it because they have forgotten that when they go from leaning forward to sitting upright in the first half of the drive, their shoulders will rise, causing their hands to rise as well—unless they consciously take steps to prevent them from doing so. As their shoulders rise, their arms should decline a bit.

---

*The phrase "level hands" is potentially misleading. When a rower rows with level hands, it doesn't mean that his left hand will be at the same height as his right; it instead means that each hand will remain the same height above the water throughout the drive, with his left hand being higher than the right the whole time.

Breaking rowers of the habit of rowing symmetrically too deep might involve simply telling them to *pull straight back* on the handles during the drive. Or it might involve telling them to attempt to row with their blades halfway out of the water. The interesting thing is that almost without exception, when a rower with a depth problem tries to do this, she will still row too deep.

In a more difficult case, it can be helpful for a rower to experience what rowing with level hands feels like. To accomplish this, I have rowers do a variation of the ten-on, ten-off drill described in chapter 6. We go out in a double, with me sitting bow. During the ten "off" strokes, I tell the rower to break my rule about staring at the horizon and instead stare at her blades to make sure they remain at flotation depth throughout the drive. During the ten "on" strokes, though, I tell her to turn her gaze back to the horizon while I give her verbal feedback about the depth of her blades. The idea is that during the ten "on" strokes, the rower will remember how her hands felt during the ten "off" strokes, making it easier for her to keep proper blade depth even when applying power.

Another drill that can help a rower overcome the tendency to row too deep is what I have called *rowing the release*: you row with your arms and back only. Row in this manner, and you will have short drives in a stable boat. This will make it possible for you to concentrate on what your hands are doing during the drive. You can, in particular, pay attention to where your hands have to be at the catch and release to keep your blades at the proper depth.

When you gain the ability to maintain proper depth during this short drive, you can try lengthening the drive by involving your legs in the stroke. At first, you will slide only part of the way toward the stern. Notice that doing this will cause your knees to rise, creating an obstacle for level-hands rowing—unless you do a proper "hands away" as part of the release. When you have successfully dealt with rising knees, you can experiment with sliding farther and farther toward the stern, being careful to keep your hands level the whole time. By doing this drill, you give your muscles an opportunity to "memorize" what the proper hand height should be during the stroke.

ROWING SHALLOW

We have seen that novice and intermediate rowers tend to row deeper than flotation depth. So, it turns out, do advanced and even elite rowers. More precisely, they tend to row deeper than flotation depth in the first part of the drive—they typically submerge about a foot of the shaft—and then rise up to nearly flotation depth for the remainder of the drive. And this, I should add, is a sensible thing for them to do. Allow me to explain why.

When you show rowers what flotation depth is and tell them that this is how deep their blades should be throughout the drive, they often protest that following this advice will leave their blades underutilized. When their blades are at flotation depth, after all, the top inch or so of them will be out of the water. But blades can propel a boat only if they are submerged, so won't rowing at flotation depth waste the top portion of the blades?

This is what I thought before I got the chance to sit behind Charlie in a double and watch him row. He rowed at flotation depth, but his blades were nevertheless submerged. This is because the pressure he put on his blade *changed the height of the waterline.* More precisely, it caused water to mound up ahead of his blade. As a result, no part of the blade was out of the water. Conclusion: rowers who try to keep their blades at "flotation depth" need not worry about having part of their blades exposed to the air.

But things are actually a bit more complicated than this. The "mound" of water doesn't start forming until the middle third of the drive. This is when the motion of the blade changes from being far-edge-first *into* the water to being surface-first *against* the water. It is therefore likely that if, in the first third of the drive, you tried to row at flotation depth, the top part of your blade would indeed be out of the water, meaning that you would fail to take full advantage of the power that portion of the stroke can provide.

In a perfect stroke, then, the blade will be deeper than flotation depth in the first part of the stroke: maybe a foot of the shaft will be submerged. Thereafter, though, the blade will rise to flotation depth.

Observant readers might now accuse me of offering contradictory advice. A page or so back, I said that a rower's goal, during the drive, should be to keep her blades at flotation depth, but now I am saying that she should start out deeper than flotation depth. What gives?

I advise rowers to "row at flotation depth" because it is my experience that rowers who row with this goal in mind usually end up with a drive like the one I am espousing: a bit below flotation depth at first, but then back up to flotation depth for the remainder of the drive. In particular, rowers who row with this goal in mind will avoid the common mistake of rowing too deep in the middle of the drive. Thus, the goal of rowing at flotation depth, although in some sense a false goal, is a useful goal to have.

If a rower wanted additional guidance on how deep the blades should be during the drive, I would abandon the row-at-flotation depth advice in favor of the following: *row as shallow as you silently can.* Listen to your oars throughout the drive. Experiment with making them shallower. When you get too shallow, your blades will tell you. If they are too shallow early in the drive, they will make a tearing noise. If they are too shallow in the middle or end of the drive, they will make a gurgling noise. When you hear either of these noises, raise your hands a bit in that part of the drive until your blades goes silent.

I should add that the fact that your blades *are* silent during the drive does not mean that you are at the proper depth: blades that are too deep will be utterly silent. What I am suggesting is that if you have noisy blades, you need to raise your hands until they go silent. And if you have silent blades, you should experiment with lowering your hands a bit during the drive to see what happens. Are they still silent? Perhaps you are rowing too deep. Try lowering your hands a bit more until there is blade noise. When you finally hear it, raise your hands to sink your blades a bit deeper. That, for you, will be proper blade depth.

FINDING A BOAT THAT FITS

Rowers need to keep in mind that although their target blade depth should be the same in every boat, how high their hands have to be held to keep them that depth will be different in different boats. Consider two boats, one a lightweight single and the other a heavyweight single. A rower will find that because the heavyweight boat rides higher in the water than the lightweight boat, he will have to hold his hands higher in the heavyweight boat than in the lightweight boat in order to keep his blades submerged during the drive.

I became acutely aware of the relationship between hand height and boat size when I was asked, for reasons that I forget, to row briefly in a quad with only one other rower in it, with me sitting bow and him sitting stroke. The boat, which was built to carry four people, rode ridiculously high in the water, and as a result, I had to hold my hands ridiculously high during my stroke. Indeed, my release targets had moved from my abdomen up to my armpits.

Even if a rower always rows the same double or quad, he might find that he has to change his hand heights depending on whom he is rowing with. If he is used to rowing a double with someone heavy, and someone light joins him for an outing, he will have to raise his hands to compensate for the fact that the boat will now ride higher in the water. (This substitution of rowers, though, should have no effect on the vertical separation between his hands.) Likewise, if he is racing a boat that takes on water during the race—perhaps a passing launch wakes him—he might find that he has to lower his hands to account for the weight of the water in the boat. And if his boat takes on enough water, he will become unable to do the recovery portion of the stroke for the simple reason that his thighs will prevent his hands from going low enough to release his blades from the water. That is pretty compelling evidence, by the way, that the time has come to stop rowing and start bailing.

Any rower must decide what boat he should row in. The standard advice is to find a boat that "fits you." The problem is that unless you have exceedingly wide hips, you will physically fit into just about any boat. You might instead try to find the right boat by weighing yourself and seeing what weight person the boat is built for. The problem here is that there seems to be no particular standard by which boat builders size their boats. What for one boatbuilder is a mid-weight would, by the standards of another boatbuilder, be a light-heavyweight.

Fortunately for rowers, there is an easy way to check the fit of a boat. They should get into it and see how far its deck is above the waterline. There should be several inches of clearance. Then they should pull their hands back to the release and let their blades find flotation depth, thereby revealing their release targets in that boat. If they are in a boat too big for them, these targets will be uncomfortably high on their abdomen; if they are in a boat too small, these targets will be way down by their hips.

BLADES AND WATER

It is hard, in a single, to see what blades do during the drive. Row bow in a big boat, though, and you will have a wonderful opportunity to watch what happens as blades and water interact. It is indeed a remarkable interaction.* In the early part of the stroke, as I have said, the blades don't so much push the water sternward as slice (horizontally) into it, far-edge first. In doing this, they move simultaneously *into* the oncoming water and *away* from the hull of the boat. This may seem like wasted motion on the part of the blade, but it generates what is called *hydrodynamic lift*, and it turns out that this is very important for propelling a boat forward.

In the middle of the drive, the blade stops slicing through the water edgewise and instead starts pushing against the water with its surface. This is when the water, because it is being pushed, starts to mound. The mound dissipates to become what rowers call a *puddle*, the outward-expanding circle of the water made by each blade. These circles persist long after the blades have left the water. Indeed, ideally what a rower will see behind her boat is the wake left by the hull of the boat with puddles on either side. These puddles should not be connected by streaks. If they are, it means that the rower is dragging her oars. And if the puddles have lesser puddles between them, it is a sign that the rower's blades are intermittently coming into contact with the water during the recovery.

It is important to realize that even though the surface of the blade is pushing *against* the water in the middle of the drive, it does not follow that it is moving *through* the water. Indeed, it is useful to watch, ideally from a bridge, as people row in still water. Note the point at which their blades enter the water and exit the water. The entry and exit points will be fairly close together, with the exit point being maybe half a meter farther from the boat than the entry point. (This would be the case if the rower had a catch angle of 65 degrees and a release angle of 45 degrees.) The thing to keep in mind, though, is that although the blade's exit point is farther *away* from the boat than its entry point, its exit point won't be very far *behind* its entry point. This is further evidence that most of the motion of the blade in the water is *perpendicular* to the boat—away from the hull during the first half of the drive and toward it during the second—and

---

*A confession: when I row bow in a double or better still, a quad, I am supposed to be either staring at the horizon or studying (in my mirror) the course ahead. I nevertheless have been known to spend time, mostly during workouts, staring instead at the way the blades of the rowers who are sitting in front of me interact with the water. Really, I have the best seat in the house for blade watching. It is my big-boat guilty pleasure.

that very little of the motion of the blade in the water is *parallel* to the boat.

Another way to convince yourself that blades don't move much face-wise through the water is to look at the puddles they make. They are round. If the blades moved face-wise through the water, one would expect these puddles to instead be oval shaped, with the long axis of the oval parallel to the hull of the boat.

Yet another way to convince yourself that blades don't move much face-wise through the water is to go to the dock, put the blade of an oar into the water, and try to move it face-wise through the water. You will find that although this is possible to do if you move the blade at a very slow speed, the faster you move it, the harder the water pushes back. Indeed, try to make a blade quickly accelerate from zero to full power, and you will find that the blade barely budges in the water. By way of contrast, it is quite easy to move the blade, far edge first, horizontally through the water.

How the blade and the water interact during the drive is hard to say. Indeed, to have a chance at figuring it out requires three-dimensional fluid dynamics modeling, which in turn requires a substantial amount of computing power.* But one thing that is clear is that the blade creates two big vortices in the water: one swirls off the far edge of the blade, and the other swirls off the near edge. There are other, lesser vortices as well.

These vortices happen to be quite powerful. The best way to appreciate their power is to row behind another boat but off to one side a bit, so the hull of your boat is passing through its puddles. Do this in a single, in calm water and behind a powerful rower, and each time your boat encounters a puddle, you will be able to feel it twitch because of the currents created by the vortices.

Besides the turbulence caused by the blades, there is the turbulence caused by the hull of the boat itself. Powerboats make sizeable bow waves. Such waves take energy to make, and therefore represent wasted energy. The hulls of racing shells are designed to avoid making bow waves, and to a remarkable extent,

---

*No one fully understands how blades and water interact, for the simple reason that no one has solved the Navier-Stokes equations that describe the motion of fluids. Solving these equations is sufficiently challenging that it is one of seven Millennium Prize problems selected by the Clay Mathematical Institute. Solve the equations, and the Institute will give you a million-dollar prize. A project, perhaps, for the off-season?

they do. Indeed, a swimming duck will routinely make a bigger bow wave than a single. There is, however, a very small wave that comes off the stern of racing shells.

I mentioned earlier that rowers should occasionally glance at their stern to make sure it isn't twitching from side to side during the drive. Rowers will also want to glance at the wave coming off the stern. They will want to see, in particular, that it stays small at the catch. If it suddenly gets bigger, it means one of two things. The first is that the rower isn't leaning forward from the waist as part of hands-away. If he instead waits till he is at the catch to lean forward, the stern of the boat will dip, and the stern wave will get bigger as a result. The second thing that can cause an increase in the size of the stern wave is if the rower rushes into the catch—which, as we have seen, is one symptom of a fear of flipping. The sudden change in his momentum when he arrives at the catch will again cause the boat's stern to dip.

Besides creating a stern wave, racing shells leave behind them a two-foot-wide zone of what I would describe as "angry water." The water in question is full of tiny vortices, brought into existence by the passage of the boat. Vortices, though, consist of moving water, and it takes energy to move water. The vortices in a boat's wake get their energy by syphoning off some of the boat's kinetic energy. If the boat's hull had no drag, such syphoning wouldn't be possible, but hulls always have drag, meaning that some of the energy rowers apply to move the boat forward must instead go to making the water angry.

In a perfect world, rowers would be able to row without making any energy-sapping vortices: there wouldn't be any in their puddles and there wouldn't be any behind their boat. Sadly, though, rowers do not inhabit a perfect world. They instead inhabit a world full of a quirky substance called "water." Given that this is so, they do the best they can.

PADDLE WHEELS AND PROPELLERS

In the early part of the drive, particularly if a rower has a big catch angle, the blades of the oars are moving primarily perpendicular to and therefore away from the hull of the boat. Many rowers reason that this sort of "outward" blade motion can't propel a boat. They therefore conclude that the early part of the drive isn't really important—that it is just the setup for the middle part of the drive, at which point the blade is moving sternward against the water, thereby pushing the boat forward. These rowers are also likely to conclude that big catch angles aren't as important as I have suggested.

The above line of reasoning is applicable to a stationary boat—more on this below—but in a moving boat, a different dynamic comes into play. Early in the drive, the blades, besides moving away from the hull, will be slicing through the water, with the blade edge farthest from the rower doing the cutting. The bigger the catch angle is, the more profound this slicing motion will be. This motion of the blades creates lift, which is remarkable for its ability to propel the boat forward. Allow me to explain.

Air flowing over the curved top surface of an airplane wing creates an area of low pressure that lifts the plane off the ground. This phenomenon is known as *aerodynamic lift*. In like fashion, water flowing over the curved surface of the back of an oar blade—ever wonder why oars have curved rather than flat blades?—creates an area of low pressure that, in effect, pulls the boat through the water. This is called *hydrodynamic lift*, and it happens primarily in the early part of the stroke, when the blade is moving far-edge-first through the water.

If you are skeptical about the possibility of "pulling on water" to move a boat, you should take a moment to consider the history of nautical propulsion. In the early 1800s, paddle wheels were how boats transferred the power of steam engines into the water. They were the obvious way to do it: if you repeatedly push water back, the ship will move forward. Then nautical engineers started coming up with designs for propellers. People wondered, quite sensibly, how blades, by moving perpendicular to a ship, could cause it to move forward. And yet ships with propellers did indeed seem to be propelled by them, so they clearly worked. But were they better?

This led to a series of tests of propeller-driven ships. They not only raced against paddle-wheel ships but did tug-of-wars against them: two ships, pointing in opposite directions, would be connected by a cable to see which could pull the hardest. The culminating event in this competition was the tug-of-war, in 1845, between the paddle-wheel steamship HMS *Alecto* and the propeller-driven steamship HMS *Rattler*. The *Rattler* won the competition, pulling the *Alecto* backward at 2.5 mph.

In modern times, the superiority of the propeller has become abundantly clear. A really fast paddle-wheel boat, even one with a powerful engine, might be able to move at 30 mph. (I found a video of a boat moving this fast, but I could find no evidence of there being an official world record for such boats.) A really fast propeller-driven boat, though, can move at 260 mph. Case closed.

Stated crudely (since I am not a nautical engineer), a paddle-wheel boat moves by pushing on water. A propeller-driven boat, by way of contrast, moves by *pulling* on water—by taking advantage, that is, of hydrodynamic lift.* If a rower derives the bulk of her power from the middle part of the drive, she will resemble a paddle-wheel steamer. If she instead learns how to tap into the power available in the first part of the drive, she will resemble a propeller-driven speedboat. One imagines that competitive rowers, presented with this choice, will want to resemble a speedboat.†

Once a rower acknowledges the contribution to boat propulsion made by the early part of the stroke, she will want to modify her rowing technique to take full advantage of it. She will want to reach far at the catch, so as to have a big catch angle. Once at the catch, she will want to plant her blades quickly; no slow catch for her. And once her blades are planted, she will want to apply power immediately with the most powerful muscles available to her—namely, her leg muscles. She will also be careful not to let this precious leg power be dissipated by shooting her slide.

An appreciation of hydrodynamic lift will also have an impact on the start a rower uses in a sprint race. Hydrodynamic

---

*The blades of propellers pull a boat through the water by creating a region of low water pressure on the bow-ward surface of the propeller blade. The reduced pressure is enough to make the water boil—to change, that is, into water vapor—even at low temperatures. (In a similar manner, at higher altitudes, a pot of water will boil at temperatures well below the "boiling point.") This is why propellers experience the phenomenon known as *cavitation*. The bubbles they produce are filled with water vapor.

†A parallel debate, by the way, arises in swimming. Are swimmers better off reaching deep on each stroke (thereby using their arms and hands as paddles) or by bending their arms at the elbows and moving their hands not only back through the water but sideways as well (thereby using their hands as propellers)? The former theory was dominant until in the 1960s, legendary swimming coach "Doc" Counsilman came out in favor of the latter theory. (Curiously, he referred to this sideways motion of the hands as a sculling motion, even though it is a different kind of "sideways" motion than the blades of oars make.) That such a sideways motion of the hands can generate lift is demonstrated by the fact that it is the motion swimmers use to keep their heads above water when treading water.

lift comes into play only when a boat is moving forward through the water; this, after all, is when the oncoming water can flow across the surface of the blade. (In much the same way, a plane's wings generate lift only when the plane is moving forward; hence, the need for a "takeoff.") In sprint races, though, rowers begin from a standing start. Thus, the goal in the first stroke or two of the start should be not so much to get the boat to full speed as to get it moving enough that the forces of hydrodynamic lift can come into play. These forces can then do a wonderful job of getting the boat up to speed. In other words, during a racing start, a rower has little choice but to use his oars as paddle wheels. His goal should therefore be to get the boat moving so he can "convert" these paddle wheels into the equivalent of propellers.

"AIR ROWING"

I should add that regardless of whether your goal is to row like a paddle-wheel boat or a propeller-driven boat, it is important that your blade be planted deep enough so that it can do its work. I mentioned, back in chapter 4, that an average skilled rower will have a catch angle of 65 degrees and a release angle of 43 degrees, for a total angle of 108 degrees. We should be careful, however, to distinguish between the total angle the blades move through during the drive, and the part of that angle during which the blades are properly submerged. If a rower has a slow catch, he might spend the first 30 degrees of the drive simply lowering the blade into the water; and if he throws water at the end of the drive, he might spend the last 20 degrees of the drive with his blade still moving sternward despite being out of the water. What is in theory a 108-degree drive is in fact 58 degrees, with 50 more degrees spent doing what might be called "air rowing." Obviously, a rower intent on winning races will want to avoid air rowing in favor of good, old-fashioned water rowing.

Stated differently, a rower with an "air drive" will end up rowing inefficiently at both ends of the drive. At the beginning of the drive, he will fail to utilize hydrodynamic lift, and at the end of the drive, he will not only fail to propel his boat but will squander the energy his oar shafts have stored up. Allow me to explain this last point.

I mentioned earlier that oar shafts are designed to flex a bit during the drive. This flexing can clearly be seen in pictures, taken from the side, of a powerful rower in the middle of her drive. This flexing may seem like a bad thing: wouldn't rigid shafts be better? The argument is that the power the shafts "absorb" when they flex isn't lost energy; it is merely stored for use later in the drive. Whatever we think of this argument, one thing is clear: if we pull our oars out of the water before the drive is over, this power will indeed be wasted. Instead of being used to give the boat a bit of extra oomph late in the drive, it will be used to throw water sternward.

RELAXING DURING THE DRIVE: THE ARMS

During the recovery, a rower will obviously be in a relaxed state, if only for a second or so. During the drive, though, he will be pulling mightily on his oars. He will be the opposite of relaxed, right?

Not really. It is a mistake to think that the drive will be all tension. To the contrary, a drive, done properly, will be a mix of tension and relaxation. Some muscle groups should remain relaxed throughout the drive. This includes, most importantly, the "shrug muscles" in a rower's shoulders. It also includes the muscles in his face: it takes energy to grimace. Other muscle groups should be active during some portions of the drive but relaxed during others. His leg muscles, for example, need to work hard during the first half of the drive but not the second. His arms, though, should have just the opposite work schedule: they need to work hard in the last half of the drive but not at all in the first half.

The somewhat paradoxical goal of the rower during the drive should be to relax as much as he can. More precisely, his goal should be not to use a muscle unless doing so contributes to the forward motion of the boat. If it doesn't, it is a waste of energy, which is bad enough. Waste enough energy, though, and you might become sufficiently tired that you catch a crab that you wouldn't otherwise have caught. Let us, therefore, consider some of the ways a rower might needlessly use muscles during the drive.

During the drive, a rower's wrists and hands should be relaxed except for the muscles at the joint of the thumb and the muscles at the last two joints of the fingers. A rower should row, in other words, with a nice, loose grip. Lots of novice rowers— and some seasoned rowers as well—don't do this. They instead clutch their handles tightly. And to find out who these rowers are, you don't need to watch them row; you need only look at the palms of their hands. They will be disfigured with blisters and calluses.

During the early part of the drive, a rower's arms should also be relaxed, meaning that her elbows should not be bent. A rower's arms, early in the drive, should play the role of ropes: they connect her shoulders to her hands. A rope cannot bend itself. Put tension on it, and it will respond by going perfectly straight. This is what a rower's arms, if relaxed, will do when the rower starts her drive.

"Breaking your elbows" early in the drive wastes significant energy. To appreciate just how much energy, try this experiment. Go to a chin-up bar and see how long you can hang there, with your elbows slightly bent. After that, try the experiment again, only this time, let your arms go slack. Even though you are tired from your first experiment, you will likely find that you can hang for much longer than you previously did.

Here is another way to think about this issue. During the drive, rowers use first their legs (and, as we have seen, a bit of their back as well), then their back, and finally their arms. Why this order, one might ask, rather than the reverse? Why not use first their arms, then their back, and finally their legs? Because doing this would put their weaker muscle groups—their arms and back—into a tug-of-war, as it were, with their strongest muscle group, their legs. It is a contest that their back and arms will surely lose. Not only that, but they will waste a significant amount of energy in the process of losing.

Why, then, do some rowers break their elbows early in the drive? They might do it in order to match their blade speed with the water speed. Unless a rower does this, as we have seen, there will be a splash. But we have also seen that there is a better way to accomplish this: "opening" her body angle a bit at the catch not only lets her match blade speed to water speed but helps prevent her from shooting her slide early in the drive.

Once a rower forms the habit of breaking her elbows, it can be hard to overcome. One drill she can do is to make a point of straight-arming—of locking her elbows—at the catch. But in doing so, she must be careful not to get into the habit of locking her elbows, since that also wastes energy. Her goal in locking them is to overcome her tendency to bend them, so she can learn to just relax them.

Another useful drill is for the rower to row with her feet out of her shoes. This will give her not only feedback on whether she is prematurely breaking her elbows but an incentive not to break them. Break her elbows prematurely, and her arms won't be able to pull very far at the end of the drive. As a result, she will find that her feet drift away from her shoes: she will experience an unsettling feeling of "weightlessness." To avoid this feeling, she will have to "save" her arms till the late stages of the drive, where their pulling will keep her feet rooted.

RELAXING DURING THE DRIVE: THE TORSO

Continuing our exploration of relaxation, we come to the shoulders. Their "shrug muscles"—the ones that raise them—should be relaxed through the drive, throughout the entire stroke, in fact. If you are rowing properly, there will be, as coaches like to say, "lots of room between your shoulders and your ears." The other set of shoulder muscles—the ones that let the shoulders move forward and back, will be involved in the drive, though. Going into the catch, the shoulders will be curled forward, and in the earliest part of the drive, they will curl back to neutral position. They will come into play again at the end of the drive, when they will curl back even farther, to provide a bit more drive length.

In an ideal drive, the back will be involved from the earliest stages: at the catch, a rower will open his body angle a bit to match blade speed to water speed and to prevent slide shooting. His back will be most active in the middle part of the drive, though: as the legs start losing their push, the back will take over as the primary source of boat propulsion.

It is instructive to contrast the operation of the legs and back during the drive. The legs will push until they can push no farther—until that is, they are straight. The back, however, doesn't do this. It could keep pulling back till the rower was lying down in the boat, but rowers instinctively realize that this would be a bad way to row. This raises an interesting question: what is the optimal amount of *layback* at the end of the drive?

Consider first a stroke with no layback at all—a stroke, in other words, in which the rower is sitting perfectly upright when she ends her drive. Such a stroke will result in a very small release angle and will therefore fail to exploit significant amounts of power. It is for this reason that the only people I have heard advocate drives without layback are people who have back problems. They worry that layback would aggravate those problems. These same individuals, though, also tend to be averse to leaning forward at the catch; once again, they want to protect their back. It is a recipe for a very short drive.

There is also such a thing as too much layback. When you push with your legs, 100 percent of that pushing will, if your back is engaged, be transmitted to the oar handles: for every inch your seat slides back, your handles will move back an inch. Likewise, when you pull with your arms, 100 percent of your pulling will be transmitted to your oar handles. This is not the case with your back, though.

The only time 100 percent of the pulling you do with your back gets transmitted to the oar handles is when you are sitting with a vertical torso. Every degree you lean back from that will result in a decrease in the percentage of the back motion that gets transmitted to the oar handles. By the time you reach the last possible degree of layback—when you go from having your shoulder blades 1 degree above the bow deck to having them resting on it—0 percent of your shoulder motion will be transmitted to the oar handles. (Your shoulder motion, after all, will be downward, not bow-ward.) Thus, when it comes to layback, rowers experience the law of diminishing returns: each additional degree of layback delivers less power than the previous degree did.

At this point, some might argue that although it is true that the back's ability to deliver power to the oar handles decreases as layback increases, one ought to take advantage of even this diminished power: some power is better than no power, right? The problem is that an extreme layback has costs that aren't outweighed by the added-power benefits to be derived from it. Allow me to describe these costs.

It is easy for the legs to recover from the drive: it takes little effort for the rower to get them ready for the next drive by sliding down the track. It is likewise easy for the arms to recover from the drive: moving hands "away" requires practically no effort. But for the back to recover from the drive, the rower must, in effect, do a sit-up. How big the sit-up is depends on how much layback there is. If you lay back only 30 degrees from vertical, you will have to sit up only those 30 degrees. If you have an extreme layback, though, you will have to do a nearly full sit-up. It will, however, take energy for you to do these "layback recovery" sit-ups. Not only that, but in the course of a sprint race, you will probably have to do 120 or 240 of them, depending, respectively, on whether you are a masters or a collegiate rower; and in head racing, you will have to do 600 of them. In other words, the bigger the layback you do, the more significant the cumulative energy cost will be.

But this isn't the only cost associated with an extreme layback. Such a layback will make it more challenging for you to release your blades from the water. Unless you can meet this challenge, you will find yourself catching crabs. Furthermore, an extreme layback will cause your body's center of mass to rise and fall significantly on each stroke. We have already explored the problems caused by rowing too deep. One of them is that it causes the boat to bob up and down, which in turn wastes energy. Realize, though, that by shifting your body's center of mass up and down, an extreme layback will also cause your boat to bob and thereby waste energy.

In conclusion, extreme laybacks come with a high price tag. And what do you get in return for the effort you invest? Very little, since as we have seen, the farther back you lay, the less effective your layback becomes, in terms of delivering power to the oar handles.

That said, I think that although having an extreme layback is hard to justify, having a greater than usual layback makes sense for some rowers. Earlier, I mentioned that female rowers tend to lean farther from the waist at the catch than male rowers. This makes sense for them to do, I argued, because it is one way that they can increase their catch angle despite their relatively short stature, relatively narrow shoulders, and relatively short arms. Judging from videos of elite rowers, though, women also tend to have greater layback at the end of their drive, and presumably for much the same reason: greater layback means a greater total angle, and by setting their foot stretchers sternward, some of this total angle will take the form of catch angle.

A Digression: Of Elbows and Ergs

In conjunction with this discussion of layback, let me say a word about the rower's elbows. They won't bend, as we have seen, until late in the drive, but when they finally do bend, *how* should they bend? In particular, should they stay close to the rower's ribs, or should they stick out to the side?

In answering this question, it is important to keep in mind the angle the forearms form with the shafts of the oars. Ideally, that angle would be 90 degrees. Think, after all, about how you use a wrench to loosen a frozen nut. You hold your forearm at a 90-degree angle to the wrench handle before you pull it, since that will deliver the most power to the nut. Throughout the rowing stroke, though, you are prevented from doing this. Indeed, at the catch, your forearms might form only a 30-degree angle with the shaft of the oar. The only time the angle approaches 90 degrees is at the end of the drive, and this will be true only if you are sticking out your elbows. So by all means, let them stick out.

Rowers often have a mistaken mental picture about what their hands do during the crossover portion of the drive and recovery. Ask them to show where their hands are when their oars are perpendicular to the boat, and they will likely hold their fists alongside each other, with the left fist to the left of the right. This is, after all, how it would look if rowing were a sensible sport. The truth of the matter, though, is that because of the crossover phenomenon, the left fist will be *to the right* of the right fist. Not only that, but the rower's forearms, rather than being parallel to each other, might be at a 70-degree angle to each other.

This, by the way, doesn't happen on an erg.* To the contrary, erg handles remain perpendicular to the erger's forearms throughout the drive. And while we are talking about differences between "rowing" on an erg and rowing on the water, consider the issue of hand height. As we have seen, it is important for rowers to keep their left hand higher than their right throughout the stroke. When people erg, though, they typically hold their two hands at the same height, so that their erg handles are level. Thus, it is possible, during erg season, to get into bad hand-height habits.

Rowers might, for example, discover that when they get back into a boat after a winter of erging, they tend to pull their hands to release targets that are the same height on their abdomen—which, as we have seen, is a bad thing. When erging, people also tend to develop "slow hands": they don't, after the release, move their hands past their knees before their knees start to bend. On an erg, slow hands aren't so bad, but in a boat, they

---

*An erg, short for *ergometer*, is a high-tech rowing machine. People sometimes race them in "ergattas," the dry-land version of regattas.

will result in oar handles that have to be lifted in the middle of the recovery, which in turn will result in blades that drag during the recovery—another bad thing.

In making these comments, I am not suggesting that rowers should avoid erging. All I am saying is that rowers who erg should keep in mind that the motions involved in erging and rowing, although similar, have some important differences and that good rowing form is a rather more complex thing than good erging form.

RELAXING DURING THE DRIVE: THE CALVES

Let us end our exploration of relaxation during the drive by considering the rower's calves. They should obviously come into play during the drive, but when? Should rowers start with their heels down and rise onto their toes only late in the drive, start with their heels down and rise onto their toes early in the drive, or start the drive "on their toes"? Kleshnev has considered this question and drawn the conclusion, on the basis of biome-chanical reasoning, that the most effective way to row is to be on your toes when you start the drive.* This is, for most rowers, the natural way to do it, since when they compress their legs at the catch, their heels will tend to lift up off the foot stretcher.

The heels shouldn't remain raised, though, since that puts the calf muscles into a pushing battle against the quadriceps, a pointless battle that will needlessly exhaust the rower's calves. Thus, shortly after the rower has commenced the drive, he should relax his calves. His heels will return to the foot stretcher, where they can act as fulcrums for the all-body levering action that will propel the boat forward.

This completes our discussion of tension and relaxation during the drive. Bottom line: a rower's goal should be carefully chosen muscle tension, thereby allowing for the greatest possible muscle relaxation. This, after all, is the most energy-efficient way to move the boat.

---

*Rowing Biomechanics Newsletter (July, 2008).

NINE

The Release

The catch is the *psychologically* most difficult part of a stroke: the rower, if he is reaching out at the catch, will be nervous about the boat flipping. The drive is the *physically* most difficult part of the stroke: it is the rower's only opportunity during the stroke to propel the boat forward, and he will exert himself mightily to do so. This brings us to the release,* which I would characterize as the *technically* most difficult part of the stroke.

The release is difficult because it involves the most dramatic motion in a stroke. A rower's hands, having accelerated through the drive, will be moving as fast toward his body as they ever will. But now that his thumbs are about to collide with his ribs, he must not only *stop* the motion of his hands but *reverse* it, and while doing this, he must feather his blades, being careful not to rotate his handles prematurely, or he will catch a crab. This is a lot to do, and there is precious little time in which to do it.

We have seen that the catch, if it causes a splash toward the bow of the boat, will act as an unwanted friction point in the stroke. The release can be a second friction point. This, after all, is where most crabs happen: it is primarily when you are trying to release your blade from the water that you can have the sensation that a wily crustacean is preventing it from rising.† If your

---

*Some coaches refer to the release as the *finish* of the stroke. I will refrain from using this terminology, inasmuch as I don't think the release *finishes* the stroke; to the contrary, it just sets the stage for the next phase of the stroke.

†The other place a crab can happen is during the drive. During that portion of the stroke, a rower can have the sensation that something, rather than preventing him from removing his blades from the water, is pulling them deeper. This can happen if a blade hits an underwater obstacle. It can also happen if, because the rower is muscling his oars or because his oarlocks are backwards, his blades are not truly square, causing them to dive during the drive. It will feel like a crab is trying to pull the blades down to his underwater lair.

release is crab-prone though, your rowing will be slow: one big crab can effectively erase the previous few strokes. And even if a release is crab-free, it will slow the boat if it is "sticky"—if, instead of rising cleanly from the water, the blades generate some backpressure and thereby check the forward progress of the boat.

A rower's thumbs, at the time of the release, should be quite close to his ribs—otherwise, he won't be fully utilizing his drive—but they should not come into contact with his abdomen. If they do, the rower will have a hard time lowering his hands to get his blades out of the water.

This is the point in the stroke, by the way, at which the clothes a rower is wearing can play a critical role. If he is wearing an oversized t-shirt, it is possible for his thumbs to catch folds of fabric, and this will interfere with his release. This is why rowers should favor "form-fitting" tops. As I like to tell my older Learn to Row students, if they need an excuse to wear Spandex despite their age, this is it.

Some rowers respond to the technical challenges presented by the release by cheating and removing their blades prematurely. These rowers lower their hands when they are still several inches from their abdomen. In some cases, rowers who do this start moving their hands sternward immediately. They are clearly wasting part of their drive. In other cases, their hands keep moving toward their body, but since their blades are out of the water, they will have eliminated the possibility of catching a crab. These rowers, in the process of wasting part of their drive, probably also throw water.

SETTING THE FOOT STRETCHERS

The first step in developing an effective release is to properly set your foot stretchers.* It is this setting, after all, that

---

*The name *foot stretcher* conjures up an image of some kind of medieval torture instrument: *stretchers*, in one sense of the word, are used to stretch shoes and boots, so wouldn't *foot stretchers* be used to stretch feet? According to the *Oxford English Dictionary*, the first recorded use of a stretcher, in the sense used by rowers, was in 1609. By 1898, the *Encyclopedia of Sport* defined a *stretcher* as "a board placed slopingly at a right angle across the boat in front of the oarsman, upon which he braces his feet." (Notice that there is no mention of shoes being attached to this board.) We also find a second nautical use of *stretcher*, though: it is the name for a crosspiece between the boat's sides. Perhaps at one time rowers used these presumably fixed crosspieces to brace their feet, before switching to adjustable foot "stretchers" like the ones we now employ.

determines how much room your hands will have in which to make the motions required to get your blades quickly and cleanly out of the water.

Rowers generally assume that where you should set your foot stretchers depends on how tall you are. What really matters, though, is not how tall you are *overall*, but how long your legs are and how big your belly is. Even though you are relatively tall, if you have relatively short legs or a relatively big belly, you might have to set your foot stretchers toward the bow end of the boat in order to make enough room for your release. A second person of exactly the same height might, because he has longer legs and a smaller belly than the first person, be able to set his foot stretchers several inches closer to the stern.

Another thing to realize is that your foot-stretcher settings will be different in different boats and can even be different in different seats of one particular (multi-seat) boat.* Thus, you shouldn't, on getting into a new boat or a new seat in an old boat, assume that you know what the proper stretcher setting will be. You should instead take a moment to figure out what setting will work best for you.

To do this, sit in the boat, put your feet in the shoes, and push with your legs until your seat is as far bow-ward as it will go. Then, sitting perfectly upright in your seat, pull your oar handles back to your abdomen. Your thumbs (which should be curled over the ends of your oars) should touch your abdomen at points several inches apart. If they are closer together than that, you need to move your foot stretchers toward your seat—or equivalently, toward the bow. (This advice, I know, might seem backwards, but remember that rowing is a backward sport.)

And what counts as "several inches apart"? In my case, I set the foot stretchers so my thumbs are about 8 inches (20 cm) apart. Experiments have shown that if my thumbs are this far apart when I am sitting perfectly upright, they will, when I am rowing, be about 12 inches (30 cm) apart at the release. (The extra 4 inches are made possible by my layback.) Twelve inches of separation means that my thumbs, at the release, will be at the outside edges of my abdomen. Indeed, if I had to pull them *past* my abdomen, I easily could.

---

*This will happen if the riggers of the boat in question are adjusted differently, with one being set relatively more bow-ward than another.

Some rowers, on hearing this last number, might be surprised: isn't 12 inches a lot of thumb separation at the release? Not really. As it so happens, there is a direct trigonometric relationship between the release angle and the distance between the rower's thumbs at the release. Given the way my oars are adjusted and my boat is rigged, a 12-inch thumb separation will give me a release angle of about 43 degrees, which, as we have seen, is average among skilled rowers. I should add that 12 inches of thumb separation also feels comfortable for me.*

Most rowers, I suspect, make the mistake of setting their foot stretchers too far toward the stern. As a result, their thumbs end up too close together at the release, which gives them not only a cramped release but a small release angle as well.

When I teach Learn to Row, I find that a surprising number of students have trouble setting their foot stretchers: even with them set as far bow-ward as they will go, the students can get only a few inches of distance between their thumbs at the release. In extreme cases—involving people with big bellies and short legs—they have *negative* distance between their thumbs: they haven't even completed crossover, meaning that the thumb of their right hand is to the left of the thumb of their left hand. Imagine trying to release your blades under these cramped conditions!

Boats, it turns out, are not designed with the needs of short-legged people—or even people with medium-length legs and big bellies—in mind. They instead seem to be designed for people who, with their long legs and slim abdomens, "look like rowers."

Where you set your foot stretchers, besides affecting your release, will affect your catch. More precisely, if you move your foot stretchers toward the stern of the boat, it will make it much easier for you—if you are brave—to reach out of the boat at the catch. Just like that, you can get a big catch angle that will let you take advantage of hydrodynamic lift.

---

*The same trigonometric relationship holds between the catch angle and the distance between the rower's thumbs at the catch. Given the way my oars are adjusted and my boat is rigged, my thumbs need to be about 34 inches (86 cm) apart at the catch in order to have a catch angle of 65 degrees, which is average among skilled rowers. I should add that to get this 34-inch thumb separation, I have to reach *way* out of the boat.

The problem with gaining catch angle in this manner is that it comes at a price. By moving your foot stretchers sternward, you will cause your thumbs to move closer together at the release, meaning that your release will become more crowded. Yes, you will have a bigger catch angle, but you might also develop a sticky release or might even start catching crabs.

Setting the foot stretchers involves making various compromises: to get something, you have to give up something. Move the stretcher sternward, and you get more catch angle but less release angle; move them bow-ward, and you get the opposite.

Another compromise involves the trim of the boat.* Changing your foot stretchers will change where your center of mass is, on average, during the stroke. Thus, move your foot stretchers toward the bow, and the bow will ride deeper in the water; move your foot stretchers toward the stern, and your bow will ride higher.† If you don't like the effect a foot stretcher setting has on the trim of your boat, though, you can compensate for it by moving your *riggers* toward the bow or stern.

And things are even more complicated than this. The tracks on which the seat slides have "stops" at both ends to prevent the seat from coming off. When you set your foot stretchers and riggers for optimal rowing, your seat might start running into one of these stops. Move your foot stretchers toward the bow, for example, and you might start hitting the bow stops before you have fully extended your legs. Rowers call this phenomenon *stopping out*. If your boat has adjustable tracks, you can deal with this problem by adjusting them. If your boat doesn't have adjustable tracks, though, or if they can't be moved to where you need them to be, you will have to change your foot stretcher and rigger settings—or move to a different boat.

In conclusion, when it comes to adjusting the foot stretchers, riggers, and tracks of a boat, rowers will find that they are faced with tradeoffs: to get something, they often have to give up something. Thus, the process of "fine tuning" a boat for optimal rowing can get quite complicated.

Trim refers to how level the boat is along its bow-to-stern axis; *set* refers to how level the boat is along its oarlock-to-oarlock axis. Trim and set are independent of one another.

†It turns out that there are rival theories on which is better, a bow that rides high or a bow that rides deep. It is a debate in which I haven't yet taken a side and hence will not attempt to settle in these pages.

CHOOSING RELEASE TARGETS

Having figured out the foot-stretcher setting that works best for her, a rower can turn her attention to the release itself and how to make it maximally effective. Although the release begins when the drive has ended, she needs to prepare for that release during the drive. In particular, she should, during the drive, be pulling her handles toward the proper release targets on her abdomen.

These release targets need to be high enough to keep her blades planted till the end of the drive. Rowers, as we have seen, can find out just how high this is by sitting in a stationary boat, moving their oars to the release, and letting their squared blades find flotation depth. Where their hands are is where, relative to their abdomen, they should be at the end of the drive.

When I have athletes use these release targets while rowing, they often complain that doing so feels unnatural. When I hear this complaint, I have a stock response: "Good! That means we are making progress." I go on to explain that rowing is an unnatural sport, meaning that if something feels unnatural, it is a good (but not infallible) sign that you are doing it right. I add that an unnatural motion, done enough times, will start to seem natural. And finally, if I am in the mood, I tell them that if their goal is to "feel natural," they shouldn't be trying to row.

If rowers do the above procedure in a properly rigged and level boat, they will find that the release target for their left hand will be a few inches higher than the release target for their right. It is important for rowers to keep this in mind. Otherwise, their innate longing for symmetry will cause them to end their drive at release targets that are equally high. Do this, though, and as we have seen, their right blade will, at the end of the drive, be deeper than their left, meaning that a downward motion of the hands that gets their left blade out of the water won't necessarily get the right blade out as well, making for a sticky release.

I should also remind readers that if they make this mistake, their boat will tell them: if their left-hand release target is too low, their left blade will gurgle at the end of the drive.

PROBLEMS AT THE RELEASE

At the release, your objective is to get the squared blades out of the water quickly and cleanly. Rowing with a sticky release is like tapping on the brakes of a car every two seconds—not a good racing strategy. More dramatically, if you lack an effective release, you are likely to catch crabs. Catch them on both sides, and you will slow your boat down considerably. Catch a crab on only one side, though, and the consequences can be even worse. It can cause you to flip your boat. And even if your boat remains upright, an asymmetrical crab can send it seriously off course. By the time you get your boat back on course, you might end up wasting more time than if you had caught a double-crab.

In an ideal release, the blades will not throw water as they emerge (although some water might pour off the bottom edges of the blades as they are feathered). Nor will the blades move sternward after they have been released: if this happens, it means that the rower has wasted some of her drive. Rather, the blades will start moving bow-ward as soon as they are out of the water—more on this in a moment. And finally, in an ideal release, the rower will feather her blades as soon as it is practicable to do so. This is because squared blades have more "sail area" than feathered blades, meaning that the quicker they are feathered, the less wind resistance they will offer.

At what moment, readers will wonder, does it become practicable to feather a released blade? It depends on the conditions in which a rower is rowing. In flat water, she can feather her blades *as they are coming out of the water*.* If a rower tries this in choppy water, though, there is a danger that blades feathered this quickly will encounter a wave. The collision between blades and wave will check the forward progress of the boat. In choppy water, it is therefore advisable for rowers to keep their blades square until they are above the water and then to feather them. Do this, and the feathered blade will likely be above any oncoming waves.

One problem with quickly feathering a released blade is that if you lack good blade control, one or both blades, on being released from the water, will immediately come back down and slap its surface. Let us call this phenomenon a *slap release*. Even if a rower subsequently gets the blades back off the water for the

---

*The idea of feathering a blade as it is emerging from the water sounds strange, but it can be done. Indeed, this was the release Charlie taught me. He told me that a blade coming out of the water should resemble "a socked foot coming out of a well-worn loafer."

rest of the recovery, the slap is not conducive to the forward progress of the boat. The obvious cure for a slap release is to keep your hands down after you have pushed them down to release the blades.

A rower who is afflicted with a slap release can cure it by doing the row-the-release drill described in chapter 7. In this drill, a rower rows with arms and back only. While doing this, she should think only about keeping her hands low after the release; doing this will keep her blades off the water. Once she cures the slap release rowing with arms and back only, she can start moving down the slide in increments. As soon as she slaps the water, though, she needs to back off a bit until she doesn't slap. Finally, she will be able to row at full slide without slapping water. She will—for the time being, at least—have taught her hands how to stay low after the release.

At the release, as in every portion of the stroke, the left blade should do what the right blade does. They should emerge from the water at the same moment, and after emerging, they should rise the same amount and feather at the same time. If one blade goes higher than the other at the release, it is probably because a rower has made the mistake of having release targets that are at the same height on his abdomen. As we have seen, this will cause his blades to be asymmetrically deep at the release, with his left blade being shallower than his right. As a result, if he pushes down the same distance with his hands at the release, his left blade will end up higher than his right.

Suppose a rower makes this mistake, and that as a result, his left blade is at flotation depth coming into the release, but his right blade is deeper than that—meaning that some of the right shaft is also submerged. Under these circumstances, the right oar will be reluctant to emerge from the water. The release will therefore cause the boat to lean to the right, and the set of the boat will be disrupted.

Suppose that instead of one blade being deeper than the other coming into the catch, both blades are too deep. Both oars will then be reluctant to emerge from the water. The rower will apply extra downward force on the handles to free them, meaning that when the shafts finally break the surface, the blades will fly upward, like breaching whales. This phenomenon is fairly common among beginning rowers.

Releasing the blades from the water will make some noise, but if the blades are symmetrical throughout the release, they will make the same noise. Thus, one clue to a defective release is when the sound a rower hears stops being "stereophonic."

When a rower does detect an asymmetry in the release, he has to determine which of his blades is misbehaving. If he decides it is both of them, then he will have to devote some serious analysis to fixing this part of his stroke. If it is only one blade that is misbehaving, though, a cure is readily available: he need only do with his bad blade what he is doing with his good blade. And he can accomplish this by letting the hand that is responsible for the bad blade mimic the hand that is responsible for the good blade.

FAST HANDS AND BODY ANGLE

Suppose you succeed in removing your blades from the water and feathering them. Some might say that this is when the recovery begins, but a case can be made that the release hasn't ended yet. You should not, at this point, stop moving your hands. If you do, you will be making the technical mistake called *pausing at the release*. Rowers, as I have explained, are unlikely to pause at the catch; because the boat is at its tippiest then, they want very much to get their blades in the water. Pausing at the release, however, is not that unusual. Even very good rowers can be seen doing it. When they do, it looks like they are pausing to admire their previous stroke, before they move on to their next.

Once you have feathered your blades at the release, you should move your hands away from your body until your arms are fully extended. Coaches call this maneuver *fast hands*, but the name is misleading, inasmuch as your hands should move away from you at about the same speed as they moved toward you at the end of the drive. Thus, during the release, your hands will make a continuous U-turn. At the end of the drive, they will be moving toward you; they will then come to a stop, drop a bit, and rotate, as you release and feather your oars; and then they will start moving away from your body. This U-turn, done properly, won't look jerky or spasmodic; it will instead look graceful.

You should not, by the way, allow your fast hands at the release to "infect" the recovery that follows: in order to row at a moderate stroke rate, your fast hands will have to be followed by a slow slide.

While your hands are moving away from you, your body should be bending forward at the waist, in order to *establish body angle*. Doing this moves your weight out of the bow of the boat. It also decreases the sail area of your body and thereby slightly diminishes its wind resistance during the recovery.

One sign that you are failing to establish body angle at the release is that the little V-shaped wave at the stern of the boat gets bigger at the catch. If you don't lean forward at the release, you will have to do so going into the catch, thereby causing the stern to dip, which in turn will amplify the stern wave. This, by the way, is a nice example of how, in rowing, what you do or fail to do in one part of a stroke can have consequences later in that stroke.

You are now ready to start rolling down the slide—ready, that is, to begin your recovery. Notice that because you have extended your arms and are leaning forward from the waist, your hands will be past your knees. Thus, when the motion of your seat down the slide causes your knees to rise, their elevation won't interfere with the motion of your hands—they will be over your shins—and won't, as a result, cause you to drag your blades.

If a rower tells me that she has problems dragging her oars during the recovery, I remind her that she can row the first half clean "for free" just by doing a proper release. If at the release she has fast hands and leans forward to establish body angle, her hands will be past her knees before she even has a chance to think about her recovery; and if she got her blades up and out of the water during that release, they likely stayed up off the water as she moved her hands forward. The second half of the recovery, to be sure, will be more challenging. This is because the boat, for reasons we have examined, becomes progressively tippier as the recovery proceeds. But still, for a rower with a serious blade-dragging problem, it will come as a relief that there is a fairly simple solution to the first half of that problem.

SURVIVAL ROWING

The above discussion of the release assumes that the boat is level at the end of the drive. If it isn't, bad things can happen. If the boat is leaning in one direction, the blade on that side will be deeper than the other and therefore harder to extract from the water. Indeed, if the boat is leaning far enough, the blade will be *impossible* to extract: the rower will push the handle of that oar as far down as he can—till it runs into his lap—but the blade will still be submerged. The result will be at least a crab and maybe even a capsized boat.

The closest I have come to capsizing a boat in a race was when a sudden gust of wind from the side tipped my boat to the right during the drive. I was taken by surprise. When I tried to get my right blade out of the water, it resisted extraction. I finally got it out, but it wasn't a pretty piece of rowing.

Another thing that can cause rowers problems at the release, even in a level boat, is waves. If a wave comes up on one side, she can raise her blades the usual amount only to find that one of them, because of the incoming wave, is still under water. At this point, her best bet is to extract the free oar, feather it, and lay it on the surface of the water, while waiting for the wave to release the other oar.

Rowing in wind and waves is a real challenge. A boat rowed in such conditions can take on water, which will cause it to ride lower and thereby make it even harder for the rower to extract her blades at the recovery. Then, all it will take is one sudden gust of wind or one rogue wave, and the rower will catch a boat-flipping crab. In particularly adverse rowing conditions, the winner of a race won't be the person who can row the fastest; it will be the person who, thanks to her ability to get her blades quickly and cleanly out of the water, gets her boat to the finish line without capsizing. She will have proved herself to be a master of what rowers call "survival rowing."

TEN

The Recovery

The release ends when the blades of the oars are out of the water and feathered, the rower's hands are in the "away" position, and she is bending forward at the waist. She can now begin the recovery component of her stroke: she can start sliding forward on her seat. In doing this, she should have four goals.

The first should be literally *to recover*—to enjoy a bit of rest. Her muscle groups should all relax. Along these lines, it is instructive to compare rowers with competitive runners. Runners get no intervals of rest during a race. Rowers, by way of contrast, get to rest on each and every stroke. Indeed, their rest interval might be longer than their drive interval. Not only that, but they get to sit down while they rest. When you consider these factors, it is amazing that people would run when they could instead row.

The rower's second goal should be to preserve the set of the boat. In order to accomplish this goal, she should try to keep her body symmetrical. Her hands, in particular, should be horizontally symmetrical, with her left hand always directly across from her right (but a few inches higher). If she breaks horizontal symmetry, after all, the oars will be at slightly different angles to the boat during the recovery, meaning that the blades will be at slightly different distances from the hull. This can have the effect of unbalancing the boat.

Her third goal should be to protect the boat speed she gained during the drive. To accomplish this goal, she must keep her blades off the water during the recovery and get them high enough off at the end of the recovery that a splash won't be kicked up when she squares them.

If a rower drags both blades, she needs to hold her hands lower during the recovery, and if she finds this difficult to do, she is probably suffering from flipophobia. If the rower drags only one blade, though, one of two things is probably happening. She might, to begin with, be letting her left hand drift too high during the recovery, causing her left blade to drag. To avoid doing this, she should make sure that she is keeping proper hand separation during the recovery. In particular, she should make sure that she lets the heel of her left hand make light contact with the knuckles of her right hand during crossover and that she goes into the catch with her left hand, although higher than her right, not too much higher.

If she does this and one blade is still dragging, then either her boat is improperly rigged, with one oarlock being too high, or her boat isn't level during the recovery. In this last case, it is probably because of an asymmetry in her body. If, for example, her torso is leaning slightly to the left, her left blade will drag. She needs, as I have said, to find and eradicate her asymmetries.

Also, in order to preserve boat speed during the recovery, she should move down the slide at a steady rate. In particular, she shouldn't accelerate as she gets closer to the catch—an action, as we have seen, that is usually a symptom of flipophobia. Doing this, after all, would necessitate a sudden deceleration *at* the catch, which in turn would check the forward motion of the boat. It would also cause the V-shaped wave off the stern of the boat to get bigger, providing visible evidence of a defective recovery.

While we are talking about protecting boat speed, a comment is in order. Most rowers assume that the boat is moving fastest at the release—at the end, that is, of the application of power that takes place during the drive. In fact, though, the boat continues to accelerate during the recovery: it surges forward in response to the rower's body moving sternward toward the catch. (The rower's body and the boat have momentum, and momentum is one of those physical quantities that must be conserved.) Hull speed therefore reaches its peak in the middle of the recovery: indeed, if you watch side-view videos of boats racing, you can see how their bows surge forward during the recovery.

Because hull drag is roughly proportional to the square of hull speed, and because hull speed is highest during the recovery, any additional drag induced at that time will have a disproportionately large impact on boat speed. This is why it is so important for rowers to keep their oars off the water during the recovery.

And by advising rowers to "row clean" during the recovery, I mean to include the beginning and end of the recovery. The feathered blade should not touch the water at the beginning of the recovery, in what I have called a slap release, and should not touch water at the end of the recovery, in what I have called a touch-and-go catch.

A rower's fourth and final goal, during the recovery, should be to set the stage for the catch. At the end of the recovery, she should flex her lower back and keep her chin high, in the manner described in chapter 8. Then, when she starts pushing with her legs, the power generated will flow through her body and into her oars, rather than being squandered making her lean forward from the waist, something she should have done back at the release.

To summarize, during the recovery, rowers should have as their guiding principle the Hippocratic Oath of medicine: first, do no harm. Don't do anything to hinder the forward motion of the boat, but other than that, enjoy your interval of rest!

ELEVEN

Putting It All Together

In the preceding chapters, we have divided the stroke into its components. We have also seen that this division is somewhat arbitrary: it is foolish to say which of these components comes first, and in a sense, it is foolish even to try to divide the stroke into components because of the way one "component" blends into another.

Although it is useful, for purposes of analysis, to divide the stroke into its components as I have done, rowers should ideally think of the stroke as an organic entity, in which each part is causally connected to all the other parts. And ideally, a rower won't be thinking, "Gosh, it is late in the drive. I had better release my oars!" In fact, while rowing, he shouldn't be thinking of his stroke at all. His stroke should be so deeply embedded in his muscle memory that it just happens. He should be on autopilot when he rows, the way he is when he walks.

To gain the ability to row as if the stroke were a single motion, though, it is helpful for rowers to focus, in their workouts, on individual components of the stroke or on what various body parts are doing during those components. I used to see Charlie out in his single, rowing up and down our river. I would ask him what he was working on. On one occasion, he said, "I'm working on pushing with my legs during the drive." This struck me, at the time, as an exceedingly strange thing to say. He had been rowing for four decades, and during that time had routinely pushed with his legs; otherwise, he wouldn't have enjoyed the rowing success he did. And yet, here was Charlie, hard at work trying to push harder and better with his legs.

More generally, Charlie told me that during his workouts, he would work on one or maybe two things. Try to focus on more than that, he said, and you will end up not focusing at all. During the workouts in question, Charlie would be quite thoughtful in his rowing, observing himself and then analyzing what he observed. But he never lost sight of the fact that this thoughtfulness was simply the price that had to be paid so that, when race day came, he could "just row"—he could row, that is, without thinking. This is certainly what a rower has to do during a race, if he is to have any chance of winning.

DESTRUCTIVE TESTING

A stroke, like a chain, is as strong as its weakest link. One thing rowers should do during workouts is find their weakest link so they can repair it. Some weak links are easy to find: they reveal themselves on nearly every stroke. Maybe the weak link is a sticky release on the left or splashing at the catch on the right.

Once a rower has dealt with these links, he can move on to weak links that, because they reveal themselves only intermittently, are harder to find. To discover these links, it is useful to engage in the rowing equivalent of what engineers call *destructive testing*: you push your stroke so hard that it breaks, just so you can see where it breaks. There are two ways to do this.

The first is to take your stroke rate up. Doing this will make some parts of your stroke easier. Your recovery, for example, won't last very long, thereby shortening the period during which you must keep the boat set. It will make other parts of your stroke harder, though. In particular, there will be precious little time to release the oars. This is why, when rowing at a high stroke rate, people become more likely to catch crabs. They also might start splashing at the catch, for the simple reason that their blade speed does not match the now-increased speed of the water.

A second way to destructively test your stroke is to get yourself very tired by rowing and then try to maintain your form. This, of course, is what happens during a race. It is instructive to compare a rower's form in the first 100 meters of the race with his form in the last 100 meters. In many cases, his latter form will be a cruel parody of his earlier form. In the beginning of the race, he looked like an Olympian. At the end of the race, he looks like Rubber Man, shooting his slide and hacking desperately at the water in an attempt to keep his boat moving. He might be glancing repeatedly over his shoulder, with a look on his face that indicates astonishment that he *still* hasn't crossed the finish line.

This, I should add, is one of the things that separate Olympic rowers from the rest of us. Olympic rowers look the same, form-wise, at the end of the race as they did at the beginning. They have the ability, in other words, to maintain their form until *the very last stroke of the race*, at which point they collapse. Good form is good, after all, because it is the most effective way to transfer power from the rower to the water. Depart from that good form, therefore, and you will be wasting energy. At the Olympic level, though, rowers cannot afford to waste even one calorie of energy.

One of the things I do in my training is 500-meter intervals: I do a timed sprint of 500 meters, row slowly to recover, and then do another sprint. I might do six sprints in a single workout. Depending on conditions, these sprints will take about 60 strokes, and as I am doing them, I keep reminding myself that the first 40 strokes are really just the setup for the final 20: it is then that I will have my most significant opportunity to work on form. Likewise, I keep reminding myself that the first five sprints in the workout are really just the setup for the sixth sprint: it is then that I will find out what part of my stroke breaks when I am really tired.

Besides wanting to find the weak links in his form, a rower will want to find the weak links in his body. When he is really tired and his form starts to break down, it is often because a single muscle group can no longer cope with the load being placed on it. Which group is it? His arms? His legs? Once he finds the group, he can take steps to strengthen it, perhaps by lifting weights.

ONE-PERCENT SOLUTIONS

I like to refer to the adjustments of rowing form that can increase boat speed by one-percent as *one-percent solutions*. Such solutions sound insignificant, but they are, for most rowers, the quickest, easiest way to increase boat speed. Realize, too, that many rowers, because their rowing form has multiple defects, can benefit from not just one but several one-percent solutions. The bottom line: take one-percent solutions seriously, and you might be able to achieve a remarkable improvement in your rowing performance.

Allow me to offer some examples of one-percent solutions. The first four are connected with the fear of flipping: stop dragging oars during the recovery, stop splashing at the catch, stop rushing to the catch, and stop catching prematurely. Thus, by overcoming our fear of flipping, we can simultaneously implement four one-percent solutions. This is why I have spent so much time talking about flipophobia. If you want to become a better rower, Job One is overcoming the fear of flipping.

Some other one-percent solutions: keep your hands horizontally symmetrical during the drive to avoid the wasted energy of a "wagging tail." Maintain proper vertical hand separation during the drive to avoid the wasted energy that results from constantly veering off course. Don't row "over the barrel" and cause your boat to bob. And clean up your release to prevent it from checking the forward progress of your boat.

There are, I realize, rowers who will be uninterested in a performance gain of "only" one percent. Any serious rower, however, should be quite interested in such a gain, particularly if all it takes to gain it is some tweaking of his rowing form. Indeed, consider a masters rower who races a single in a 1000-meter sprint. If he can improve his boat speed by a mere eight-tenths of one percent, he will, by the end of the race, have gained one boat length. (In other words, in a singles 1000-meter race between two rowers, the one who is eight-tenths of a percent faster than the other will finish one boat length ahead.) In a 2000-meter sprint, it will take only a four-tenths of one percent improvement in boat speed to gain a boat length, and in a 5000-meter head race, it will take a mere one-sixth of one percent of improvement to gain a boat length. In this last case, improve your performance by one full percent, and you will gain *six* boat lengths over the course of the race.

Instead of expressing the effect of improved boat speed in terms of boat lengths gained, we can express it in terms of elapsed time. A non-elite masters rower might row a 1000-meter sprint in 4 minutes. If he could have increased his boat speed by one percent, he would shave 2.4 seconds off this time (since 2.4 seconds is one percent of 240 seconds), and 2.4 seconds is huge, even in non-elite racing. In many of the races I have been in, shaving this much off my elapsed time would have gained me multiple places in the outcome of the race. And in head racing, the effect on elapsed time is even greater. If it takes you 20 minutes to row the course, a one-percent improvement in boat speed will reduce your elapsed time by 12 seconds. Rowers should, in other words, care very much about one-percent solutions. Indeed, they should be obsessive with respect to them.

BETTER THAN GOOD

It isn't hard to find rowers, even seriously competitive rowers, who aren't form-obsessed. These rowers tend to fall into two categories. There are, to begin with, rowers who think that if you row a lot, form will take care of itself. This *can* happen, especially if the rowing involves lots of self-observation and subsequent reflection on what has been observed. Row a lot without self-observation, though, and your rowing will accomplish little more than to embed bad habits deep into your muscle memory.

The second category of form-resistant rowers might be called the "no pain, no gain" school. They are convinced that the key to rowing well is to be very strong and to possess enormous stamina. Such rowers tend to judge the quality of a workout by how tired they are when they get off the water. Are they wobbly-legged when they step out of the boat? Good! Are they still tired two days after finishing a workout? Good! These rowers have little patience for spending workout time on form-improvement activities.

There are two problems with this approach to rowing. The first is that the stronger you get, the harder it is to get stronger still. Thus, for someone who is very strong, it will be vastly "cheaper" to improve his boat speed by improving his rowing form than by trying to become even stronger than he is. The second problem is that the choice between working on form and working on strength is an example of what logicians call a *false dichotomy*: you don't have to choose between them since it is possible to work on both at the same time. There is therefore no excuse to work on strength and ignore form.

To gain and maintain good rowing form, rowers are well advised to spend time doing the drills I have described in this book. (See the appendix for a listing of these drills.) Olympians might spend one-third or even one-half of their workout time maintaining or improving their rowing technique. If the best rowers in the world think it worthwhile to do form-work, surely someone who is rowing at the intermediate level can benefit from doing it.

It is wonderful for rowers, when they are trying to acquire or maintain good rowing form, to have a knowledgeable and experienced coach to guide them. If they don't have such a coach, though, they need to learn how to self-coach: they need to learn how to observe their rowing and on the basis of their observations, find and correct the mistakes in their rowing form. It is my sincere hope that this book will be a useful tool in helping them in these efforts.

Appendix: Rowing Drills

Name	Description	Propose
Glide at hands-away	Move to "hands-away" position; let the boat glide until a blade starts dragging on the water	Detect asymmetries in the release or in body posture early in the recovery
Glide at the catch	Move to the catch position, keeping the oars feathered; let the boat glide until a blade starts dragging on the water	Detect asymmetries in body posture late in the recovery; overcome the fear of flipping
Tap at hands-away	In a stationary boat, sit at hands-away position and bob the blades into and out of the water repeatedly	Develop the ability to maintain body symmetry early in the recovery
Tap at the catch	In a stationary boat, sit at the catch position and bob the blades into and out of the water repeatedly	Develop the ability to maintain body symmetry late in the recovery; overcome the fear of flipping
Sliding tap	In a stationary boat, sit at hands-away and start bobbing the blades into and out of the water; keep doing this as you slide toward catch position and then slide back to hands-away	Transition from the tap-at-hands-away drill to the tap-at-the-catch drill
Sideways tap	The same as the tap-at-hands-away drill but done with the boat turned sideways to oncoming waves	Develop the ability to maintain body symmetry early in the recovery; overcome the fear of flipping

Name	Description	Purpose
Pause at hands-away	Like the glide-at-hands-away drill except that you start rowing again before an oar touches the water	Develop the ability to maintain body symmetry early in the recovery
Pause at the catch	Like the glide-at-the-catch drill except that you start rowing again before an oar touches the water; during the pause, your blades should be feathered	Develop the ability to maintain body symmetry late in the recovery; overcome the fear of flipping
Low stroke-rate rowing	Row at an abnormally low stroke rate, maybe as low as 12 or even 10 strokes per minute	Develop your ability to keep the boat set during the recovery; overcome rushed recovery
Slow-motion rowing	Row at a normal stroke rate, but at low power; you are really just going through the motions of rowing	Develop your confidence at the catch
Ten-on, ten-off	Row with proper form at low power for ten strokes; then try to retain that form while increasing the power for ten strokes	Develop your ability to retain form at high power output
Perfection drill	See how many strokes you can do before you have a defective stroke	Detect intermittent mistakes in your rowing form
Rowing the catch	Release your blades before you are halfway done with the drive; then move back to the catch and take another stroke	Overcome splashing at the catch
Rowing the release	Row with your arms and back only	Overcome release problems, including a sticky release and a slap release
Straight-arm rowing	Row full strokes but without breaking your elbows	Overcome bent elbows early in the drive
Shoeless rowing	Row with your feet out of the shoes	Overcome bent elbows early in the drive

Acknowledgments

I want to take this opportunity to thank the people at Greater Dayton Rowing Association who have become my river family. Club members who played pivotal roles in my development as a rower include Peggy Nicodemus, my Learn to Row instructor all those years ago; Chris Luhn, Doug Barker, and Linda Clemens for their valuable advice; Lou Franca and Ben Boehm, elite rowers both, for showing me how to take my rowing to a higher level; club president Jim Wall, who had the wisdom to realize that I would be more effective as Adult Coach than as Adult Director, particularly since the latter post did not involve film-making; and all the big-boat crews that kindly let me occupy a seat in their boat—and especially, the rowers who sat one seat bow-ward of me in those boats, back in the days when my splash problem was at its worst.

Thanks to Alison Bour for proofreading the manuscript of this book.

Thanks as well to all the Greater Dayton Learn to Row students who have let me teach them and all the competitive rowers who have let me coach them. These rowers provided me with the equivalent of a post-graduate education in sculling, and I suspect that I learned far more from them than they learned from me.

A special thanks goes to Michael McCarty who, by tolerating the dozens—or was it hundreds?—of experiments I came up with for us to try in our double, played an important role in my sculling education; and thanks to Michael as well for all the support and encouragement he has given me over the years.

I would end my list of acknowledgments by thanking my rowing mentor Charlie Doyle, had I not already attempted to do so by writing this book.

Index

Made in the USA
Coppell, TX
03 October 2020